KELSI'S FOOTPRINTS

This is my story...
This is God's Glory!!!

Library of Congress Control Number: 2015911392

ISBN-13: 978-0692481981
ISBN-10: 0692481982

Published by:
DewDrop Publishing: PO box 564 Ladson SC 29456
www.facebook.com/Kelsisfootprints

Scripture quotations are used from the New International Version; Public Domain.

Special Thanks To:

First of all God; for showing me the way.

My family; for sharing my pain.

Rev. Clark; for speaking to me for God.

My friends and coworkers; for
supporting me mentally and financially
during this time.

My daughter Morgan and her father; for helping
me through my healing process.

Mary Neilson; for typing the words I wrote.

May God bless you all!

Table of Contents

Introduction

***

I come from what we call "normal" nowadays: a divorced dysfunctional family. Nevertheless, we had our problems, but we have always been a very close and loving family. I have one brother, Steve, whom we call "Bubba," and three sisters, Denise, Patsy and April. I also was blessed with a step sister and brother; Chrissy and Ryan. Together through many family issues we have grown closer than many families would ever dream of. My mother, Marie has always devoted her life to her children. Without a doubt, she has always been there for us. My father, James was always there, but just never as up close and personal as our mom. I live now in a small town called Summerville, just outside of Charleston, South Carolina. Other than my brother, most of my family resides within minutes all around me.

I have a very close lifelong friend whom I really consider as family because we are truly soul mates that have crossed paths by God's fate. Tanya has experienced many of the same upsets in life as I have. Therefore, we have always been great support for each other.

Mike, who is Kelsi's father, was mostly the type of person that would live day by day, free spirit. I on the other hand, was more on the reserve side. It was fun or should I say…different for awhile with Mike. He liked to enjoy life, and that was my attraction. We became pregnant during our time together; we were both young and just not prepared for this stage in life.

This book was inspired by a dream I had one night. In the dream was this Bible verse:

(Ecclesiastes 12:10) The teacher searched for just the right words and what he wrote was upright and true.

I am not writing this book to gain your sympathy for my loss, but to in some way, help those of you who have walked in my shoes, to find comfort and peace through God.

*Some names have been changed to protect the innocent.

Dreams change that we had
planned, but we **have to accept**.

Wisdom comes in forms we don't
always want, but **have to learn.**

Learning to live without someone is
not within our ability alone,
but we **have to let go.**

NDC

Chapter 1
My Pregnancy

Planned or Unplanned

***

I was twenty-one years old and had been working at a Chrysler dealership in town since high school. That is where I met Mike. He worked at the car detailing shop down the road where we sent our cars to be cleaned. We dated for a while, went out a lot, and then decided to move in together.

I loved the idea of being together as a couple, playing house. I know all I ever wanted was to have a family. But that was far from what Mike wanted at the time. We never talked about trying to get pregnant, but we both knew that I was going to stop taking the pill because it was causing me to have problems. We never took any other precautions to keep from getting pregnant. I knew part of me really wouldn't mind and just maybe a part of him didn't mind either. As time went by, we were still going out, partying and having fun. We moved a lot because Mike had changed jobs.

I started to worry because it had been months since I had been off birth control and I was still not pregnant. Then one day, Mike and I went camping with Tanya and her husband. It was a gorgeous weekend; Tanya and I were just sitting out by the campsite relaxing, talking about life and whatever else, while the guys went to rent a boat, which we later went out on.

Having so much fun, when I look back now, I feel sure this was the day of Kelsi's conception.

Even though I was in the midst of being a free spirit that day, that now was a glorious day for me, and I say this only because of who I am and where I am now, that day was a turning point for a new life for me. Sure enough, within the next month, I missed my cycle.

I was excited but I knew that with my past history of cycles it wasn't uncommon for me to miss a cycle. So I waited a few days. But being too eager, I couldn't wait any longer. I rushed out for a home pregnancy test. After I did the test, Mike and I waited anxiously.

The test results were positive. I was scared, but excited and Mike said he was happy. So I told my family and they were happy. My Mom, on the other hand not really being crazy about our relationship was worried.

Just as most moms would be, but she gave me her support anyway. I figured it was best to call my doctor, whom I had been using for many years to set up an appointment to be confirmed.

I am not really sure why I thought I was ready for this adventure in life. Having a baby I knew was a huge commitment. All I knew was I that I was happy about being pregnant.

My First Appointment

***

It was June 24, 1993. I was so excited and nervous at the same time. I just could not wait to go to the doctor. So there I was sitting in the waiting room trying to pass the few minutes that felt like an hour by, glancing at magazines. All the time wondering, "Okay, what are they going to do? Is everything going to be okay?" This was the first time I had ever been pregnant, so I had a lot to learn. Other than your friends and your sisters telling you their childbirth stories, you don't have a clue. Finally, the nurse came and called my name. So down the hall we went. First, I had to have my weight checked, then a urine sample and blood pressure.

Then they took me to a room to wait for the doctor. I usually had to wait a few minutes on the doctor when I came in for a visit. Dr. Amber was my doctor. She is part of a four women practice. She is very well known and highly recommended. She always has lots of patients.

The other women in the practice were also very good doctors, whom I would meet in my upcoming months.

Doctor Amber knocked on the door to signal her arrival and in she came. Pleasant and cheery as always, she greeted me. Then she said my test was positive and I was approximately 6 weeks pregnant. I had a mixture of feelings; the one with the most weight was happiness. Dr. Amber asked me a few questions and what my plans were, and told me briefly what to expect during the next few months. She congratulated me and said my estimated due date was around February 14th. Then we went back to the nurse's station, where the nurses gave me some videos and pamphlets and my next appointment date. On the way home, I had some time to think. I knew I was happy about the baby. I was just unsure about how Mike really felt. Only because I knew that our relationship had never been on a permanent foundation.

Nevertheless, I knew I would be fine with or without Mike. But, coming from divorced parents, that was the last thing I wanted for my child. I knew I always had my family to lean on.

So I came home excited and told my family and Mike that it was confirmed and that I was due in February.

My sisters were excited, my brother and my mom hesitant, but supportive. You see, my brother Steve had taken the role of being like a father figure to me when I was younger through our parents divorce. So he was concerned for my well-being I know.

Mike seemed happy. Finally, I felt like my life was going to have completeness and meaning.

A few days later, Mike went out with one of his friends and stayed out all night. I knew then that he was not ready and that he was very unsure of this baby in our life.

Treasured Pictures

***

My pregnancy seemed to be pretty normal. In the next few months' nausea and vomiting was a way of life. I continued to work without any problems. I was so excited and nervous at the same time of what this pregnancy had in store for me. I ate a lot of fruit and vegetables. I took my prenatal vitamins. I went for walks around the apartment complex we lived in. I didn't go out or drink anymore.

I tried to do everything I could think of that was healthy for the baby and me. Before I knew it, I was starting to show.

Every month when I went in for my appointment they measured my stomach to see how much the baby was growing. They always checked my weight and asked how I had been feeling. I always loved it when they listened for the heartbeat. It was reality, hearing your baby's tiny heart beating so fast, an awesome reality. Nothing could be more perfect. I met a few of the other doctors in the practice; they all seemed to be nice and knowledgeable. Most of all, they said I was fine and the baby was doing fine. The days seemed to drag on by. Mike and I argued a lot, because he was not settled with this.

I was unhappy and worried because I never knew what the next day would bring where we were concerned. I continued to hang in there. So I just continued to work everyday to pay what bills I could and believe that things would change with him when the baby was born. I was really excited about my next office visit, it was my first ultrasound, I don't recall fore sure, but I believe Mike was with me. No one else around me existed when the nurse hooked up the ultrasound machine.

There was nothing but my baby and me. I was five months along. You could see everything, tiny arms and legs and the tiniest heart beating. It was miraculous and overwhelming. It's like meeting your baby before it's born. I didn't want to know the sex of the baby; I wanted it to be a surprise. Dr. Amber gave me several pictures that day of the ultrasound.

Those pictures, I will treasure forever.

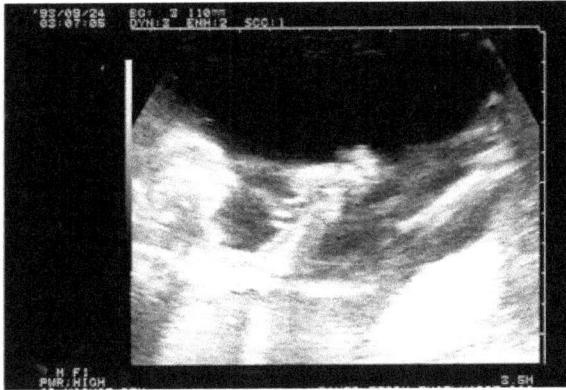

Tanya my best friend was also pregnant at the same time I was. Only she was due in April and I was due in February. She brought me a special frame that had a teddy bear attached to it for the ultrasound picture. It was really neat both of us being so close and pregnant at the same time. We talked a lot about how our babies would be the same age and that they would grow up to be like siblings, go to the same schools and be in the same classes just like we were. It always gave us something to look forward to. Every once in a while instead of going to my doctor's appointment alone, I would take my sister or my niece, Billi Jo, so that they could hear the heartbeat.

Chapter 2
Separation

Major Changes

***

The time was going by, day by day. I was getting bigger and more uncomfortable. Mike was living life as he felt, so we had to reserve money where we could. And I really wanted to start fixing up a baby room.

But I knew we wouldn't be in the apartment we were in much longer. Mike was the maintenance person at the apartment complex and that job was not really what we needed financially.

The autumn season was upon us and the holidays would soon follow and we were in a lot of trouble financially. My mom had a house for rent. So she let Mike and I move in for next to nothing for rent. Mike got a job at a detail shop not far from where I worked. So we rode together and I dropped him off on my way to work.

Things seemed to settle down for a while. Mike was staying home and we were getting along. Right before

Thanksgiving, my Aunts were visiting from out of town so my mom wanted us to all get together and so we decided to do it at my house.

Mike was going to do the cooking on the grill but then a friend called and needed help moving some things, so Mike said he wouldn't be gone long, took our only vehicle and left. I was angry and told him he should have told his friend to wait until later, but he left anyway.

Nevertheless, my family came and we cooked and had a great time as we always do. My Aunts are all wonderful; they are all like mothers to me. It grew later, and later, finally everyone left and went home. I was getting really angry. Mike never returned that night. I was all alone, pregnant and had no way of going anywhere and furious. So, I called my sister, April. She and my niece, Rachel came to stay with me.

I was so hurt that he would not care enough about me and our baby to leave us stranded.

I cried and cried to my sister and niece for hours. Then finally the phone rang. I'm not sure what time it was, but it was my father. At that time, my father was going out a lot and obviously ran into Mike somewhere and Mike knew I would not be happy and just maybe I wouldn't mind if he were with my dad.

So my dad says, "Nickie, Mike's here with me and he's going to stay here tonight, he'll be okay." I was furious!

First of all, my dad is supposed to protect me, not him. Second, Mike was just being irresponsible and I had enough. I was very upset for Mike involving my dad in our problem. When Mike got on the phone, I told him if he didn't come home, he would be sorry.

So after all that, I was beside myself. I was very upset; I didn't feel the baby move. I couldn't calm down. I knew then that this was very unhealthy for the baby. Something had to be done. I finally calmed down and lay awake for half the night deciding what to do.

So I decided it was time to end this childless relationship. My baby deserved better. So that next morning I got up and packed my clothes and hid the suitcase under the bed.

I told my sister she could go ahead and leave when Mike came in. Sometime around noon, Mike came home.

He came in the front door with a Christmas tree.

This was his attempt of making amends for his selfish behavior. I don't even remember what he said. I said nothing. I waited for him to get in the shower.

Then I threw the suitcase in the back of the truck and I left. My sister was behind me. I knew there was nothing else to discuss. So I went to my mom's apartment.

After the next few days, and a lot of thinking I decided to take one of Mike's calls. We talked about the situation and decided it was not going to work this way.

So the plan was for him to go to up north and live with his dad, get a job and save money, enough money to get our own place by the time the baby was born in February.

I was going to stay in South Carolina with my mom until the baby was born.

So here it was the very beginning of December, Mike was leaving to go to Pittsburgh to start a life there so the baby and I could come there to live and have our little family work out. I really hoped that he would get a job there and get us a home and save money when he could.

But at that time my eyes were still closed to Mike not being ready for this. I wanted to give him the benefit of the doubt.

Now, first of all I did not want to have a new baby and leave my family to move across many states, but I thought I would give it a try. And I knew that I could always come home.

Growing Closer

***

Well here I was getting settled in my mom's apartment. My mom of course was glad to have me. It was early December and I was about 30 weeks (7 1/2 months). Everything had been fine at the last couple of checkups (October and November). I was still working every day at Hoover Chrysler. They were very good to me about any time I took off. Usually after work I would come home and my mom would cook this huge wonderful dinner.

My favorite of course was fried chicken, butter beans, rice and occasionally, macaroni and cheese. That she would cook a lot. Sometimes I would tell her I was tired of fried chicken and I would make some hamburger helper. But some how an hour after eating that hamburger helper I always found my way to Mom's fried chicken. Needless to say, I was really starting to put on some pounds with my pregnancy. It was wonderful through. My mom and I spent a lot of time together, talking about things in our past and growing closer.

We got along so well now that I was a woman instead of the rebellious teenager that once gave her so much trouble. Every once in a while we even went out shopping together for baby stuff. It was so special being there in her care. It was comforting and safe.

But of course, when I told her my plans to move to Pittsburgh when the baby was born, she was hurt and asked me if I was crazy. Mike and I talked several times a week. He got a job detailing cars at a dealership and was supposedly saving money.

He did send me a little money to pay on our percent of the doctor's bill. His focus for our finances was supposed to be on a truck for us to have 2 vehicles and a place to rent. So I paid the bills here with my money.

I really enjoyed staying with my mom. I remember putting up some Christmas decoration's with my mom, thinking to myself deep down, I would go to Pittsburgh when the baby was born to make an attempt at having this family work; and that if it didn't I would be back with my baby to stay with my mom.

This month of pregnancy was really memorable for me though. The baby was so big now; it felt weird to feel its movements so strong.

One time I could actually feel the imprint of the baby's butt on the left side of my stomach sticking out. I think back on that day now…. How priceless that moment was.

What was really funny was our family decided we were all going to get our family pictures taken since my brother was in town from Greenville, SC. We were doing the grandchildren in one pose and the siblings were in a separate portrait.

I was standing in the back by my brother and my sister, Patsy was sitting in front of me or should I say my belly and because like all pictures you have to move in close, we couldn't help but laugh because the baby kept kicking Patsy in the back of the head, since her head was level with my belly. It was a funny and special moment.

My brother, Steve and my sisters, Denise, Patsy and
April were all very close, but Patsy and I have always had a
special closeness. I don't know why, we just do. She
volunteered to be my Lamaze partner, as it was time to
have one and I didn't. So we signed up for the class along
with Tanya and her husband and another friend of ours,
Cathy and Jamie. It was once a week on Wednesdays for
about 8 weeks.

It was a lot of fun, all of us in the same class. We did
more cutting up than learning. It was very helpful for me,
laughing with my friends took my mind off the fact that my
real partner, the father, wasn't there. So I tried to
concentrate on Christmas being around the corner. It was
now the beginning of December.

My mother and I spent even more time together getting ready for the holiday. Shopping for presents, of course! I was pretty big by now. I was about 32 weeks along. It was getting pretty exciting for me. I always loved Christmas.

The closer Christmas got, the sooner my baby would be here. I was still working everyday. My job was a very busy job, but I was sitting at a computer so it was not strenuous for me to work. Patsy went with me every week to Lamaze classes.

My monthly checkup was coming up on December 15, and I was anxious because I was so far along and I just loved to hear the baby's heartbeat. So my older sister, Denise, planned to go with me to my appointment.

I took the day off and we went to the doctor's office. At this point in my pregnancy I had already met 3 out of the 4 doctors and was pleased with all of them.

Today I was meeting with Dr. Daniels, the only one I had not met yet. So, when they called me back I went through the same routine. Blood pressure check, urine sample and so forth.

Then Denise and I waited in the room. Dr. Daniels

came in and introduced herself, measured my stomach, checked the baby's heartbeat, started writing in the chart and asked me if I had been having any problems. I said no and she said, "We'll see you back in a few weeks," and left the room.

Neither Denise nor I were impressed. I was upset because she was in such a hurry I didn't feel fully examined. But we just figured she was either too busy or having a bad day and left it at that.

I was sure everything was normal because Dr. Daniels would have been alarmed if it wasn't. So I tried to set my mind at ease. We all expect miracles from doctors as if they were God. But the truth is, they are human also and they get busy and sometimes they can make mistakes.

We all condemn them when they do. As if they were supernatural. But we all need to remember that they are not God. God is the only one who can and will perform miracles.

Sometimes he may use a particular person to do so, but it is only by God's grace that it happens. Dr. Daniels did what she was supposed to do for my check up; she just was not a personable doctor.

This time during my pregnancy was extra special for me. Spending quality time with my mom, sharing the Lamaze classes with Patsy and Denise being able to attend the doctor appointments. Really meant a lot to me

It was getting close to Christmas and my mom and I had to finish decorating the apartment. The night we put up the Christmas tree was so special to me. Usually all of us kids get together and put up the tree together as a family. But, since my brother moved away, we didn't do that very often anymore. So this time, just my mom and I put the tree up. I remember talking with her as we hung the ornaments about all kinds of things.

But, I also remember thinking, "this time next year my baby will be helping us." I was so happy and content that night. It was very calming. Even though deep down I really thought no matter what I tried, things probably would not work out with Mike and I.

I really hated the fact that the baby might not have a father around. Not that Mike would never be there; just that he would remain living up north. I had enough love for my baby, and I wasn't going to let that thought ruin the holidays or that peaceful night.

I knew no matter what, as close as my family was and as the days grew closer for the baby to arrive we would be fine.

I talked to Mike every week, he even sent a Christmas present in the mail. Patsy and I were still going to the Lamaze classes. And I was starting to get prepared for the baby to be here.

Christmas with my family was great as usual. And as always, just as soon as it came ~ it went.

After New Year's it was back to our daily routine. The excitement of the holidays was over.

I had a bigger excitement and it was getting closer and closer. My due date was February 14 but one of the last times I had a check up with Dr. Amber, she said I might be a couple of weeks earlier with the baby. So it would be January…… and it wasn't long now.

The Baby Shower

***

So here it was, the big day, my baby shower. I was so excited. I had waited for this day what seemed like forever. It was Saturday, January 15, 1994. I had a lot of things I wanted to do that day. My sisters had planned the shower for the evening. Patsy was the Resident Manager at an apartment complex in North Charleston so it was going to be in her apartment. So that morning my niece, Billi Jo, who was 9, had spent the night with me and we decided that morning to go do some shopping.

Billi Jo and I had always been very close since she was a baby, we had always had a special bond, and we always spent a lot of time together. We spent the day shopping. I don't really recall what we were shopping for, but we made a day of it while my sisters prepared for the shower. Sharing that day with my niece was very special to me.

It was about time for the shower, so we went home to get ready. When I got to my sisters it was so lovely.

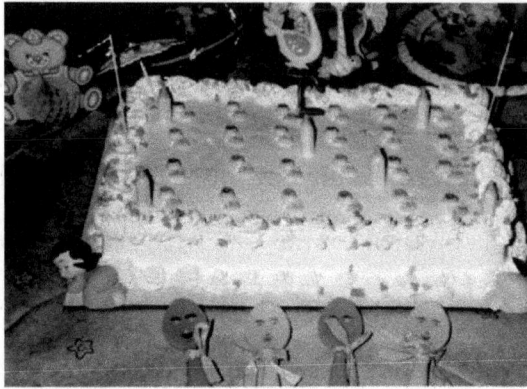

They had a pretty cake with a baby boy angel and a baby girl angel and pink and blue booties (I wanted to be surprised so I didn't want to know the sex of my baby). There also were balloons and hanging decorations. Wow, I thought, this is all for me. Some of my friends started arriving.

All three of my sisters were there, along with my mom and step-mom. My best friends Tanya and Wanda and my cousin, Gail and other family were all there. Most of the girls I worked with at Hoover Chrysler came from both stores. We had lots of fun, of course, playing crazy games, laughing and joking. There were so many gifts! I received some wonderful things. After we opened the gifts, we had lots of food to snack on, so several of us stood around talking. Some of the guests started to leave.

After most everyone left, just my mom, my sisters, my friend Tanya and my cousin Gail were hanging out talking. It was around nine o'clock and I remember it like yesterday. Gail, my cousin was standing in the doorway of the living room talking and as she was talking I started to feel very hot and faint.

So, as she was talking, I kept kind of slipping back towards the stairs, away from everyone, just to sit down to cool off. I'm not sure who it was, but one of them asked me if I was okay. I said, "No, I don't feel well, I need to lie down." At that point I just felt so sick and faint. So they helped me upstairs to lie down. Almost immediately, it seemed that after I lay down, I started having cramps in the top of my stomach. My cousin Gail and Tanya went home and my mom and Denise stayed with Patsy and me.

I was so nervous; I had a million things going through my head. This is it! Can I do it? Will I freak out? Mike is in Pittsburgh! What if I'm too early! I just couldn't calm down.

I had never been pregnant before so I had no clue as to

what contractions felt like and where they usually occurred. All I knew was the top of my stomach felt like it was ripping apart. My sisters stayed right beside me, helping me breathe.

I was lying on my sister, Patsy's bed. No matter how I tried to breathe, the pain didn't seem to ease.

But it was not steady like every 3 minutes or every 5 minutes. It was more like an ongoing cramp. I'm not sure what time it was, but hours had gone by and neither my sisters nor my mom or I had gotten any sleep.

So we decided to call the doctor because the pain didn't let up. So when we called Dr. Daniels was on call and we told her where the pain was and she asked how for apart the cramps were. We told her it wasn't consecutive and she said to time it and if it was consecutive, to call her back.

The pain never subsided to every few minutes. It was just an aching, tearing feeling. Nevertheless, it continued through the night. I tried to take a shower to ease the pain. Also, I tried different ways of lying down. Nothing seemed to make it go away. So into the wee hours of the morning I decided to try sitting upright in the recliner.

That seemed to ease the pain somewhat. My mom was downstairs with me. She kept asking me if I was still hurting and was very concerned. At this point my sisters were upstairs trying to get some sleep. As I sat there in the recliner, I was so tired but worried.

The pain would stop long enough for me to doze off for maybe 10 to 15 minutes then a sharp pain would run through the top of my stomach and wake me instantly. This went on for several more hours, of which were the early hours of the morning.

The pain would was so sharp through the top of my stomach, almost like a bolt of electricity, taking my breath until it let up.

My family and I just thought I was in labor. I had thought about calling Mike in Pittsburgh to let him know what was going on but I figured it being Saturday, he might be out, so I would call the next day. I think it was around 8:30 a.m. Sunday morning when the phone rang, it was Dr. Daniels.

She was doing a follow up on my call that night. She asked me how I was feeling. I told her we did not call back because the contractions (so I thought) were never a certain number of minutes apart, that it was more so a pain on the top of my stomach that would not ease up through the night, but had eased a little when I sat upright. I tried to describe to her what I felt the best I could.

She told me to just get ready and come in to the hospital so she could check me. So my mother, sisters and I got up and started to get ready to go to the hospital. I was nervous, but at this point, riding in the car on the way to the hospital….. I was hopeful and excited.

Excited, I guess, just thinking I was in labor and it would be soon that I held my baby. The severe pain was pretty much gone at this point.

Of course the pain eased, since I was going to the hospital. Besides being really sore around my stomach and my back hurting, I only felt a few times in my stomach a tightening feeling on the way to the hospital.

I think everyone was excited, no one was complaining about being tired.

When we arrived at the hospital, Dr. Daniels came right out to get me and take me back. I took my mother with me.

Dr. Daniels took us in an exam room to quickly brief with us again what was going on. I told her again of my pain in the top of my stomach and that I had not felt the baby move all night.

So she asked my mom to step out with her so I could undress and she could check me.

She came back in, she examined me, said I had not dilated nor thinned out and there was no bleeding. Then she listened through her stethoscope to the heartbeat and said everything sounded fine.

Then she waited outside so that I could get dressed and to get my mother.

She explained to us that it was obviously false labor and gave me a prescription for a sleeping pill called Seconal to help me rest at night.

She said that Dr. Barker was coming in to take over her shift and if I had any more labor pains or if any bleeding occurred to call back.

Needless to say, I was disappointed. My mom and I

met my sisters in the hallway. They were very surprised to see me out so soon. The whole exam took approximately 10 minutes in all. I felt like she had checked for everything, so I just told my sisters what she said and we all went home. My mom and I went back to her apartment, after we loaded up everything from the shower.

I was very tired and sore so I rested all day. I knew I had to work the next day so I tried to get some sleep. I was still so sore and certain ways that I laid or turned, that pain would come back in the top of my stomach.

So I found some comfort laying on my mom's couch with the heating pad on my back and my body laying half on my right side, so that's when I halfway slept.

The pharmacist did not have the medicine Dr. Daniels had prescribed for me so I did without.

At some point I called Mike to let him know what was going on. I was very unsettled. I just kept thinking about how twice now I had met with Dr. Daniels and she had been very rushed.

But I just knew she had done what she was supposed to do. My belief was that she did all she needed to do to make sure all was ok at that moment.

There was no bleeding and the heartbeat was fine she said. I just was being very sensitive. So I figured I would just call in to the office in the morning. Monday morning came; I still felt very sore and over tired, so I called in to my job and stayed home that day.

They were always very good to me, my boss said "no problem," when I told him what was going on. After that, I called in to Dr. Amber's office. They put me on hold for Dr. Amber's nurse.

They always would ask your name and your doctor and put you on hold for the nurse.

I remember when she answered the phone, she said "Hello, this is such and such, Dr. Amber's nurse, how can I help you?" I didn't catch her name but I caught Dr. Amber's nurse.

There were so many nurses that you see on all your visits, it's hard to remember their names.

So, I briefly told her about coming in on the previous Sunday morning for labor pains. She was very quiet and then asked what time and when.

She said she had no record of it and I told her about my prescription and I also said I still had not felt the baby move.

She did not seem alarmed. She told me to call around to other drug stores for the Seconal and if I couldn't find it to try some Benadryl. Then she scheduled me to come in on that Thursday to see Dr. Amber.

She said it was time for me to come weekly, as I was around 37-38 weeks. So, I felt content with that. I had been worried about the baby not moving, since before it was so active. But, I had told Dr. Daniels and now, Dr. Amber's nurse. I assumed they heard me and it was no big deal; that it was normal. I guess I should have made them respond to my statement.

Chapter 3
The Beginning of the End

Devastation

***

The week seemed to be slowly dragging by. I continued to sleep on the couch every night. I still was in a lot of pain. It was bearable, but certain ways I moved really hurt. The soreness seemed to surround my stomach. I stayed out of work most of the week. On Wednesday, Patsy and I had the Lamaze class to attend. So that evening I really felt like getting out so we went.

It was very important to me to attend all the classes to learn everything I could. So I could hopefully keep control over my pain during delivery. We went to class and that particular night, we were doing a floor exercise. We were all talking and laughing at all of the silly positions the instructor had us in.

During all of this, I remember my stomach making this loud gurgling noise. Not a growl like being hungry, but gurgling so loud that several people looked back at me.

I thought it even felt a little different than your normal growl from hunger pains. Then, I just thought that I was a little on edge about everything that had been going on and I left my mind at ease because I knew that the next morning, Thursday, I was scheduled to see Dr. Amber. Then she would explain to me why I had been having so much pain in the top of my stomach and why the baby was so still.

I figured it was all a part of being close to the end, your body getting ready. Or even False Labor? So I thought.

The next morning came and I felt like I needed to go to work. I was way behind in my paperwork. So I went in since my doctor's appointment was for that afternoon. I did some filing and caught up on some computer work. As the day progressed, the pain in my stomach seemed to intensify.

Tanya was working that day in the office with me. I had been training her to do my job while I was out on maternity leave. Her baby was not due until mid April. She kept telling me to sit down. But I needed to stand, because it hurt in between my chest and stomach if my posture was not straight.

She also kept asking me if I wanted her to go with me to the doctor. I said, "No, I would be okay." She had missed a lot of work herself being pregnant. I did not want to cause her to miss anymore time.

Besides, somebody in my family had accompanied me to every doctor visit. Just this one time no one did. My appointment was at three o'clock, so I decided to go ahead and drive over. A part of me was excited to think she may say, "Okay we will have to put you in the hospital and induce."

The other part of me was in so much pain that it made me nervous to the point that I felt that something was not right. So, I drove over, thinking all the way. I didn't have to wait long after I got there. They took me back and I was waiting for Dr. Amber. I was so thankful to be seeing her that day. She came into the room cheerful as always. She always made me feel comfortable.

She asked me how I had been. So I told her about coming into the hospital over the weekend and how I had been feeling. As I was talking, she motioned for me to lie back, so I did.

She proceeded to check for the heartbeat with her stethoscope. She then told me to stay still for a minute she was going to get the ultrasound machine. She left the room, got the machine and was right back. She hooked it up and started running it across my stomach. Then she asked me if I had any family with me. At this point, I was getting very scared. I just answered, "No." Then I said, "Why, what's wrong? Is something wrong?"

Dr. Amber was very hesitant and tried to delay the answer as she continued to look at the Ultrasound machine.

She had no choice, she just replied, cautiously *"Your baby….. has died."* --- *There's no heartbeat!!!!* She proceeded to point to the screen where the heart was and that it was not beating. Terror rolled through my body like thunder. I started screaming and crying and I couldn't stop. Every time I closed my eyes, all I saw was my life in total darkness. "Oh, God, no," I screamed. "This cannot be real. Not my baby……WHY?" Dr. Amber answered, sympathetically "I don't know."

Then she took my hand as I was screaming, helped me rise up off the table and hugged me…. then led me out of the room down the hall to her office.

Through the halls all the nurses and other patients were just standing there looking down or with a somber look. Oh, they knew what had happened because I could not stop screaming. Things quickly went in to a whirl wind from there.

In her office, she sat me down and picked up the phone to call my mother. I remember her saying "Ms. Dew, this is Dr. Amber here. I've got Nickie here in my office and she paused.... She has lost the baby and I need you to come to her as quickly as possible. All the while I was crying uncontrollably. She hung up with my mother and then she said, I'm going to give you a few minutes alone and I want to speak with Dr. Daniels about the weekend. I'll be back," and she left the room.

Leave me alone for a few minutes, I thought? I was already alone, I felt. I knew I needed to call Mike in Pittsburgh. I wanted him to be there as soon as possible. I kept picking up the phone, and I would get so upset, I couldn't remember the number, so I would hang it up again. I just could not get myself together. So I decided I needed to call Jeremy, Mike's brother, he worked near the doctor's office; he could be there with me. I changed my mind again; I knew I needed to call Tanya.

She was at home so I called there and her husband answered. All I could get out of my mouth was, "Let me speak to Tanya." She grabbed the phone knowing something was wrong. I just started to cry harder and said, "The baby died." She gasp and said, "I'll be right there." We hung up. Then I tried to breathe and calm down a little. I remember pacing around, sitting down, only to get up and pace some more.

My head felt like hours had gone by, but it was only minutes. I remember gazing out her office window, looking out at the trees and the sky. I didn't see anything but a voice in my head said, "God is the only one that can help you through this." Right then I knew… this storm was coming. There was no mistake! This *was* happening, to me! So I calmed down enough to remember the number in Pittsburgh where Mike worked. When I called there, his father Luke answered the phone. They worked together at the same dealership.

Luke was a salesperson and Mike was the auto detailer. Luke knew something was wrong by my voice. I did not tell him, I felt that I had to tell Mike first.

Before I lost control again, Mike came to the phone. "Hey, what's wrong?" he said. I started crying when I heard his voice. I said, "You have to come back here, something happened to the baby, the doctor said the baby was dead." I heard him drop the phone, I'm sure in shock, and he picked the phone back up and said he would be here tonight. I was crying too hard to answer any questions.

All this took place in minutes. Dr. Amber came back in the room and said she had spoken with Dr. Daniels. There was no obvious problem at the hospital. Then, in came my mother and niece, Billi Jo. Then shortly after that, my sisters Patsy and Denise also Tanya, with her husband, Brian arrived. We were all crying and holding each other. It was like saying Goodbye forever.

Then, Dr. Amber asked me when I wanted to go to the hospital, because she was going to have to induce labor. I could go that night or wait until early the next morning, which was Friday. In my mind, I was thinking I cannot make any decision right now ~ God, I can't even breathe. But that was only the first decision I had to make with many more to follow. This was coming to pass.

So I knew I was beside myself along with my family and I wanted Mike there so I decided to wait until morning. Then I asked Dr. Amber what was going to happen with the delivery. I said, "There is no way I can go through all of the physical pain of labor for nothing!" I knew I couldn't handle that so I asked her to do a C-section. But, she didn't want to do that because of a higher risk of infection and a lot longer healing process. She said she would run a continuous drip of epidural.

She pretty much guaranteed I would not feel any pain. I only wished that medication would stop my heart from shattering over and over inside. Then my mother asked Dr. Amber "Wasn't there something she could do to bring the baby back after delivery? And for one second... I looked up at Dr. Amber in the hope that our technology could do such a Godly miracle. But she just shook her head no.

I just wanted to fall asleep and wake up from this nightmare. Dr. Amber went ahead and scheduled the delivery with the hospital for the next morning, Friday, **January 21, 1994**. *A day that would be burnt into my heart forever.*

Dr. Amber told me how sorry she was for me and hugged me with tear filled eyes. With that, my family and I got up to leave to go home and prepare for the days to come. As we walked down the hall to the side door sobbing and crying and holding each other, it seemed like everyone was staring at me.

We all drove back to my mother's apartment. My aunts and cousins started coming in later that evening to see me. I have a very extremely close family and when a tragedy strikes we pour together and help in anyway we can. Sometimes just by being there. My mind was numb to everything that was going on.

Almost like my body was just sitting on the couch watching everything and everybody as my mind hovered above thinking, "Why is everyone here for me? There's nothing wrong with me, I'm fine. Go home, I'm fine." Then I would keep slipping back into reality. Like once, I remember Patsy, my sister, telling me when we were leaving Dr. Amber's office, that Tanya, my closest friend, (who was also pregnant) was walking beside her crying and said, "Why Nickie? Why didn't God take mine, I already have two?" I was so shocked that she had said that. I know that she had always been there for me, but it takes a special friend to say such a thing whether they truly mean it or not. Those are big words.

As the evening drew to a close, most of my family went home to prepare for the next day. There might have been a few people still there besides my mother and me. I was in and out of my mind. I was waiting for Mike to get there. His brother Jeremy was picking him up at the airport and bringing him over. I remember crying for a while then being solace, then start crying again.

I was in such disbelief. This was not at all what I had planned. "What had I done?" Where and how could I go on without my baby? I was totally petrified of the next minute, the next hour, days, years, and my life without my baby that I had longed for, prayed for and thanked God for.

I remember throughout the evening several people asking me questions. I recall answering them, but mostly with no emotion. Have you ever been hurt somewhere so bad that the pain just goes numb because your body goes into shock and numbs the area and your mind? That was me!

Finally Mike and his brother arrived. I think it was close to 9 or 10 o'clock. His brother hugged me with such sorrow. Not knowing what to say towards the situation he told me how sorry he was and that he would see me the next day at the hospital. Mike and I went to my room upstairs.

He had a lot of questions of course. I answered them as best as I could. The only question I recall him asking specifically was the same thing my mother had asked, "Can't they do something? " I remember standing there, looking and feeling my stomach, thinking this was the last night with my baby.

Then for one moment I imagined a way to keep my baby, by just staying pregnant. I know it was crazy, but I was desperate. I knew that could not happen. Then I remember lying on the bed next to Mike as he rubbed by stomach. I was glad he was there.

I wanted him to feel my pain. After all this was his child also. Surely he had his fears as well. As we laid there I don't recall much talking, mostly we both were thinking about the next morning. How was I going to do this? I was hurting so bad inside and so, so afraid. I had never had a baby before and I was afraid of that alone.

But more so my baby was not going to be alive. God, what would I do when I looked at my baby? Would I be able to deal with it? Could Dr. Amber have made a mistake? As I dozed off, little did I know the worst was yet to come.

The Birth-Day

***

January 21, 1994, it was early in the morning. I had to be at the hospital at seven o'clock. We all got up, my mom, Mike and I. My brother Steve and his wife Lyn were there. Lyn was also pregnant, about 7 months; I don't know how she dealt with what was going on. I am sure it probably terrified her.

I took a shower, got dressed and tried to hold my emotions in and be strong. But I was so sick to my stomach. Thinking about what this day would hold. My mom tried to get me to eat; I remember eating about a half of a piece of dry toast.

Then I remember my sisters Patsy and Denise arriving, along with Tanya and her husband to go the hospital.

No one was saying anything; there was nothing to be said. We were all afraid. Everyone just stayed in their cars and waited for me, Mike and my mom to start off to the hospital. It was a long, quiet drive. All the while I was waiting to wake up. Please God, wake me up!

Don't let this be real, I can't do this. All this was going

through my mind. I said nothing, I held it all in. I'm sure some of the same things were going through my family's minds, as well.

We arrived at the hospital, my heart started racing heavily. It took everything in me to set one foot in front of the other. This was it! It was no dream!! This was it.

As we got inside the hospital and someone went up to the check in nurse, an attending nurse came out immediately. She was overly nice. She introduced herself and then pulled up a wheelchair.

When I sat down, I lost it. I couldn't hold it in any longer. It really slammed me, I had no way out. I remember looking up at my family like someone PLEASE help me out of this.

They were all crying because they couldn't take it away. This was only the first of many tears we would shed. The nurse tried to assure me that she would take good care of me and that everything would be all right.

As she wheeled me on to my room and the nurses proceeded to set me up, my mind was so overloaded with fear and my heart shattered with pain, something in me started to go numb. I just lay there on the bed watching the nurses whirling around the room. They were all so nice, and all had been informed of what was going on.

Dr. Amber arrived and I remember her talking to me, telling me that she was going to monitor me from her office most of the day. She was going to start the epidural drip for the pain and the Pitocin to induce the labor, that it would probably be most of the day. But she told me to report to the nurses if I felt any pain.

I don't remember saying much or having any questions. As I sat up on the bed so the nurse could start the epidural, I leaned against my sister Patsy; I never even flinched as she placed it in my back. I was almost lifeless inside, there was nothing anyone could do to cause any more pain than I already felt and I had a long day ahead.

As the hours started passing by the nurses were in and out. Some of my family stayed in the room with me at all times. The rest were in the waiting room. Mike was in and out. The phone kept ringing, flowers kept arriving and I kept dozing in and out.

The medicine was kicking in and making me dopey. I

needed a lot of rest. The nurses would bring in papers for me to sign from time to time. I remember them explaining what the papers were but I just signed without much thought to most of them.

As the day proceeded, I never felt much pain other than in my heart. I remember being asleep and Dr. Amber coming in to wake me up and tell me she was going to break my water. It was everything I could do to stay awake, but I remember feeling a pressure release as she broke my water. I remember looking up at Tanya, because she was holding one hand as Patsy held the other, and saying what a relief. It felt like 20 pounds had been lifted. As the hours turned into the early evening, the medicine had me really out of it. Thank God!

Half of the time I didn't know what was going on. The nurses came in and out to check my blood pressure and everything else, and then I would doze back off. Finally, I was awakened once again shortly after four o'clock by Dr. Amber tapping on my leg. I remember looking up at her and she said it's time to push.

My mind was so drugged I just wanted to go back to

sleep. I recall her getting me in position and tapping my leg from time to time saying "Wake up and push." Tanya and Patsy were by my side and my sister Denise and Mike stood off to the side of the room.

I remember looking back and calling Denise just to make sure she was there. I also recall the tears streaming down her face. I began trying to push. I tried and tried but I was so weak and tired and I wasn't coherent. So I heard my sister sigh and try to start talking to me as Dr. Amber was talking to the nurse. I knew she was sending for the forceps because I could not push as I could not feel my lower body. I didn't care, let them do whatever.

My life was over the very minute she told me my baby was dead anyway. I wasn't in much shape to realize what was happening with all of the medicine in me, nor did I feel much as Dr. Amber used the forceps. After a few minutes, my baby was delivered at 5:00 p.m.

Everything was silent. It was the most devastating silence in the history of my life. No monitors, no baby crying…………….. Just silence!

Dr. Amber did not hand the baby to me, but to the

nurse. I had to know, so I asked "What is it?" "A girl," she said, "7 lbs. 6 oz." I don't even remember what all went through my mind. Every inch of my body and soul was numb. Everything seemed to move fast from here. They had taken my baby girl to have her cleaned up. Meantime, they had to get me situated. They stopped the medicine and got me cleaned up. I remember somebody coming in to ask me if I was ready to see her. I said yes. I was lying in my bed, so my sister lifted the bed.

Everyone was in the room, my brother, Steve, my sisters, my mom, Tanya and a couple of my Aunts. Mike was somewhere in the crowd. So here came the nurse with my baby. I couldn't see her in the baby basket. So my mom asked if I wanted to hold her. I quickly shook my head NO; as I knew I wouldn't be able to let go. Then weeping loudly, my mom asked if she could hold her. I shook my head yes, for I couldn't speak. As my mom held her she faced towards me so I could see her face. She was so beautiful, the prettiest pink skin and tiny bright red lips.

I remember just staring at her and feeling tears run down my face, until I could look no more. So, I just turned my head, thinking why and how can this be? Then the nurse took her back out of the room. So many things were going on in my head. I was afraid to hold her because I would not be able to let go. Why? Just what ever could be the reason for my baby not to have breath in her body?

I just wanted to close my eyes and never breathe again. I never knew such a love until I looked in her face. Nor did I ever know such pain until I looked in her face, the face of an angel.

****

****

****

After a couple of hours, I remember the nurse telling me I had to get up to go to the rest room. I couldn't walk, my legs were still weak. So she tried to wheel me in the wheelchair. Thank God my sister, Denise was with me. I kept passing out.

In the next few hours my feeling came back and I was in excruciating pain in my stomach. I assumed it was from the forceps that had to be used. So the nurses went to get some pain medicine. During all of this, my dad came in. I remember the look on his face, he couldn't even speak. His baby girl dealing with something he could not take away.

I was in so much pain I could not be still. The nurses were in and out again with paperwork that needed my signature. One was to release my baby's body to the funeral home. Others were to give her a name and, etc. I had already chosen a name before any of this nightmare came about. Kelsi Lauren was to be her name.

A name that would ring like church bells in my ears for the rest of my life. I remember Dr. Amber asking me if I was sure I wanted to release her body to the funeral home because I may want to see her again. I said no, I did not think I could handle seeing her once more.

I am thankful however for Dr. Amber had taken it upon herself to take a few Polaroid pictures of her. Those are all I have to this day. The hurt that consumed my heart ~ my soul ~ my mind and every inch of my body was unbearable, greater than any pain I had ever known. It wasn't long before I heard someone saying that the funeral home had arrived for her body. It was 9 o'clock that night.

I was afraid to see her again because I remember Dr.

Amber also saying that Kelsi had been dead for four to five days and that when the air hits her body, it would start to deteriorate. I did not want to take that chance. I wanted to remember the baby girl I saw. It was very hard for me to comprehend that I had carried her for four to five day's dead and I did not know. But, now I know that is why I did not feel her moving.

Everyone started to go home. Both of my sisters, Denise and Patsy and of course, Mike were all staying. They were all not leaving my side. I was so thankful. I did not want to be alone. That night we all dozed off; me in my bed and them in cots all around the room. I remember waking up because I had to use the rest room, and I felt tears coming down my face.

I realized I was crying and I did not even know it. I was so hurt inside and my body was so numb, my soul was crying. So I was real quiet and I sat up and looked around at my sisters and Mike. I did not want to wake them up because I just wanted to cry silently. I still did not have complete feeling back in my legs so I had to walk carefully to the restroom.

After I dozed off for the rest of the night, daylight brought another day. I opened my eyes to the light and just started screaming. Patsy and Denise came running to my bedside. I just looked at them and cried "I want my baby." The pain was even more real now that all the drugs had worn off. My chest felt like all of my life had seeped out of it and at the same time it felt like weights were sitting upon it like I was stifling; no breath.

No matter how hard I try, I will never completely be able to describe the pain that engulfed me that very moment.

I would never wish it on my worst enemy. Patsy and Denise did not know what to say or do, but hold me and cry. There was nothing more they could do. I just wanted to die. I could not deal with this; I just wanted Kelsi, my baby. This was hell that I have woke up to. Not a nightmare but my reality, my private hell. I had no clue of how I was going to deal with this.

From Planning a Nursery to a Funeral

***

It was Saturday, January 22, 1994, the day after her birth. I was supposed to be excited on bringing my baby home and enjoying the nursery with all the baby gadgets and so forth. But the plans had been cruelly changed. Now I was now trying to put together a funeral. Throughout the day my family and friends came in and out to visit.

I was still so weak and the pain was forever real in my heart. When I had to shower, both my sisters never hesitated, one held me up while the other washed my body. They cried the whole time... sometimes the power of unconditional love will take your breath away. I am beyond expression on how they had such strength for me.

My mom came in sometime throughout the day; she had been on the phone with the funeral home. I know she hated to ask or talk to me about it but the truth was ~ I had a lot of decisions to make. The funeral home wanted to have the funeral the next day because of how long she had been dead, and her body was not in the best condition. But there was no way I could do that. I had to have time to get my thoughts together and some strength back.

So I told my mom she had to speak with them about it. There still was a lot of things to be discussed like a dress for her burial, a casket, vault and of course, money. As I'm worried about all these things, my mom told me that during all this that my co-workers had taken up an offering to help me in my situation. They had collected around $1500.00, which was an enormous help.

I was so thankful for that. For I had no savings and this was just not in my plans for having a baby. My aunt knew the people at the funeral home, from losing loved ones in the family, so she talked to them about helping me financially however they could. I hated to put this all on them, but I really had no choice, I needed their help. Sometime, throughout the day, the attending physician was Dr. Barker and she had come in to discharge me.

She asked me how I felt and if I was ready to go home. I wasn't ready to go home. I was weak, sore and couldn't walk, but besides all of that, the main reason I wasn't ready to go was I couldn't bear the thought of leaving the hospital with empty arms. I know I had a lot to do with the funeral, but I was not ready, so she said that was fine. They still had me on Darvocet for pain and it caused me to sleep a lot. Everything was going so fast, my mind was racing. For the rest of the evening and through the night I just slept off and on. It felt good to sleep because when I was sleeping I wasn't aware of my heart aching so badly. I hoped I would sleep forever, but I kept waking up, only to face the nightmare all over again. The next day, Sunday, January 23, I knew I would have to go home. So Dr. Barker came in to see how I was.

She offered her condolences once again, and gave me a list of things to do to take care of myself and all my prescriptions for pain. My sisters, Patsy and Denise were there for they had spent the night again. My best friend, Tanya was coming so that I could ride with her, she had a van. I needed something that I could lay down in or keep my legs lifted. From the waist down I was very sore, from the forceps and delivery. Dr. Baker returned to release me after lunch. She gave me my discharge papers and the nurse came with a wheelchair. As Mike wheeled me down the halls, Tanya, my sisters and the nurse were walking with us.

As we approached the automatic doors and they opened, the fresh air hit my face, with the sunlight. I looked down towards my lap, and the emptiness began to seep into my chest. On the way home I remember Tanya and her husband, Brian, trying to make me smile or laugh. I remember laughing a couple of times, but it hurt to laugh. When I laughed, my soul was silent, as if it were dead. Now I know the true meaning of a "Broken Spirit."

It's almost like when your heart is so hurt from pain you can't actually feel the difference between your outer self and inner self. As I've heard it said by a famous Speaker of Women of Faith, "You're smiling on the outside but screaming on the inside." There's a time before the inner screaming where your spirit is silent. Because it is numb from the shock. That's how I was on this day and several more to come.

After I got home, there were lots of decisions still to make. There was family coming in and out. Friends and people from our church brought all kinds of food and words of comfort. The funeral had been planned for the coming Tuesday, January 25. So we decided that first thing Monday morning we would go to pick out the casket, dress and whatever else came up. So, for the rest of the evening I tried to rest, for I had a busy next day. Mike's sister-in-law, Hanna, dropped by to see me. She herself had several miscarriages, early on in her pregnancies. She told me as she sat down beside my bed how sorry she was for me.

Then she handed me a present, it was a mother owl with its wing over a baby owl. She said that in her family it was tradition, when someone lost a baby, they give a present to that person if they had been in those shoes, so they would know they were not alone. Little did she know, how much that meant to me and how much it helped me at that very moment, and years to come….because I did feel alone.

All these people were coming in and out saying things to comfort me as if they knew how I felt. But they didn't know. Yes, they felt sorry for me and they didn't really know what to say. But she did.

Even though hers were miscarriages and I was full-term, they were wanted and real. Hanna helped me feel like I wasn't the only one on the earth with empty arms. The next morning, Monday, January 24th came and I was still not ready to do what I had to do. I had no choice. I wanted to make sure the last and only things I could pick for my daughter were exactly perfect. First on the agenda was going to the funeral home and picking out a casket and to the cemetery to pick out a plot.

So Mike and I, along with my mother, his mother and my sisters, brother and aunt all met at the funeral home to go over all the arrangements. As we sat in this room and the funeral director went over all the details of what would take place at what time, it was so unreal to take it all in. Mike and I had to sign papers for this and that, approve this and that. It was all too much. Then it was time to pick out the casket. This was the moment I had been dreading.

I knew we did not have much money, but I knew that I would want something that looked "perfect" like she was. As we were walking through the room, with all of the displays, all of these thoughts were going through my mind, how can I be standing here! This is where my baby's body is going to lie. Then, after the director pointed out a few that weren't acceptable, I saw it. The very one she would lie at rest in. It was so tiny. It was a small, pink satin casket lined with ribbons and tiny pink roses. It just jumped out at me.

I couldn't even speak; I was so taken by everything. I just stared at it. My sister noticed I was gazing at this particular one, so she said, "Nickie, do you like this one? It's beautiful." I shook my head yes, I didn't care about the price, then I said, "That is the one," as I felt tears coming down my face along with chills down my spine.

So on with the next on the list was the cemetery plot. My uncle and cousin were buried at a beautiful cemetery just on the outskirts of town. So that's where I wanted Kelsi to be; close and by our loved ones. After that we had to order flowers, for the service was the next day. So of course, I looked for the most unique and perfect one. Part of the day was gone and my body was still weak and I had already been on my feet more that day than I should have, so they got me a wheelchair to ride in because I was feeling faint. Probably, both mentally and physically, and I still had more to do.

We decided at the funeral home that instead of buying a

vault for Kelsi, my aunt owned a metal shop and my
cousins offered to make Kelsi one. I thought that would be
extra special so Mike decided to help them with it. So we
went home to eat dinner and after, Mike was off to help
with the vault and I was off to the mall with my sisters and
Mike's mom Deanna to pick out a dress for Kelsi to wear.
I was looking for the "perfect" dress and shoes. After all, it
had to be a dress for an angel.

They wheeled me around to several stores pointing out
this dress and that one. Then, finally, there it was solid
white with satin and lace.

Just what an angel would wear. Then I found the prettiest pair of white satin shoes with pink flowers to go with it. I was content with that. Then we went back home to gather everything together to take to the funeral home for Kelsi. So we laid everything out on the bed so we could get pictures of it. Her dress and shoes, a blanket, a small teddy bear, and a special ring Tanya had bought for her.

As I stood there looking at this stuff while my sister took pictures for me, I just thought, "This is it? This is what it comes down to what she gets?" Everything I had planned for her beautiful nursery. All she needed was right here on a corner of my bed.

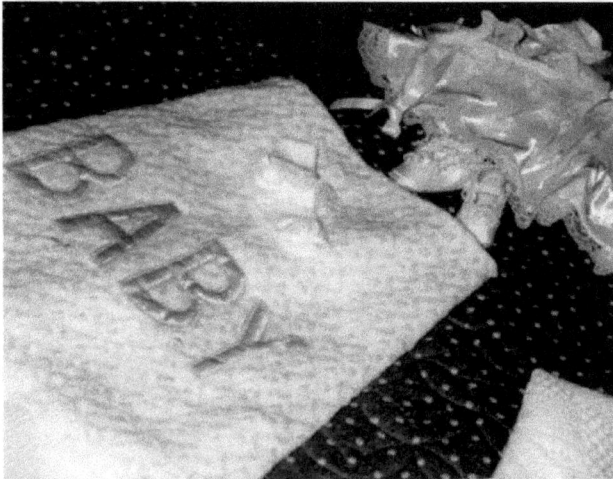

So we rushed down to the funeral home before it got too late. I handed the man all of her things and thought to myself, I can't even dress her, not even once. I had stayed so busy most of the day, I didn't have time to stop and cry. Everything had to be perfect. After all, these were the only things I would ever be able to give her.

I walked through the halls on the way out and I wondered what room she was in and debated on just going to get her and run. I didn't know where to, but I would just run. Not that it would change anything, but that my arms wouldn't be so empty.

The next morning came just as soon as my eyes closed, it seemed. The funeral was in a few hours. They stopped by with the vault before they took it to the cemetery. It was so special. They had engraved her name, Kelsi Lauren upon it. My very close cousins Blake and Clint along with Mike had made this special for her..... How priceless!

I was overwhelmed with the support of my family, Mike's family, my coworkers and my friends that were showering me with open arms.

I was not attending a church at that time. I had gone to my mother's church a few times so her Pastor was going to perform the service. I was a nervous wreck, closer and closer to the time to go.

Mike and I rode alone to the funeral. There was no talking, I cried the whole way, feeling sick to my stomach. When we arrived, I couldn't believe my eyes.

There were cars everywhere, people standing all around, and flowers upon flowers. Everyone from both car dealerships I worked at with an exception for a few left to keep them open was there for me. On top of friends from school I hadn't seen in years, all of my family and several of Mike's family.

I got out of the car and tried to walk, but I got dizzy. I just couldn't take it all in. So, Mike got the wheelchair and took me over to the gravesite. I don't remember what the preacher said, I just kept crying and staring at her casket thinking, "my baby" is in there.

Lord, anytime, please wake me up or take me out! I just wanted to get to that casket and hold her and love her and make her wake up!

I never knew that one person could cry so many tears. Everyone was crying; there were no dry eyes. After the service, everyone lined up to offer their condolences. That meant so much, seeing everyone care so deeply.

I couldn't believe this was it; this was the place I would come to when I wanted to visit Kelsi for the rest of my life.

After everyone left the chapel, my family and I went back out to see the grave. I completely lost it. I just started screaming, "I want my baby."

At this point, we were all at a loss for words. I could not bare the fact that my baby was in that grave. How on God's earth could I go on from here? My life was useless, I was devastated; no meaning left.

Chapter 4
Grief Recovery

Emotion Overload

***

In the empty days following the funeral, it was really tough. Life had to resume back to normal for everyone. Everybody had to go back to work. The visits from family members and friends started to slow down. Not that they did not care or think about me, but they had their own lives to maintain, while I had begun to try to make sense of mine.

Thank God my oldest sister, Denise was not working at this time, so she came over almost every day to sit with me. I still had to get better physically, my body had been through a lot and it needed time to heal, so I didn't go out much for the first couple of weeks. Mike had to go back to Pittsburgh after the first couple of weeks. So my plan was to go up and stay with him as soon as Dr. Amber released me on my first check-up.

My mind seemed to race all day about everything that

had taken place. It drove me crazy sometimes. I was so thankful when my mother would come home from work in the evening. I never told her, but sometimes I really just wanted her to hold me like she did when I was a hurt child, her arms around me and her prayers over my wound always made me feel so much better and at peace. I just wanted to feel that again. Any peace, any sense of comfort, I longed for. Deep down I knew that even though she was my mother and it may help for a few moments, this wound was way too big for even her to heal.

After I went to my final check up and Dr. Amber released me, I took off to be with Mike in Pittsburgh. A part of me really needed him, so I thought. He was Kelsi's father; surely he could help me through this pain. After I arrived in Pittsburgh, I shortly found things were not what I was expecting. Nothing had been worked out to our plan. He had a job, but no home for us to live in. He was living with his father. We fought all the time and I was miserable. I stayed for a little while, then left and came home to my moms. I would stay at my moms for a week or two then would drive back to Pittsburgh. Nothing I was doing was working. I made that trip back and forth several times; once in the middle of the night during a bad tropical storm. Finally my family knew I was going to kill myself if I continued the way I was. They got together and confronted me with what I was doing and my mother told me she would not let me leave again and that I was going to go with her to counseling. Oh boy was I angry and rebellious! But they did stop me and I went to counseling. Some time passed and Mike and I never seen each other again.

At first, I felt lost, sad and alone. These feelings play in together because when you are lost, you are alone and that brings sadness. I didn't really know what to do with my arms that had programmed themselves to be holding a baby.

(Isaiah 41:10) So do not fear, for I am with you do not be dismayed, for I am your God

(Isaiah 43:2) Fear not for I have redeemed you, I have summoned you by name, you are mine. When you pass through the waters I will be with you. And when you pass through the rivers they will not sweep over

you. When you walk through the fires you will not be burned.

(Joshua 1:9) Have I not commanded you be strong and courageous; Do not be terrified; do not be discouraged for the Lord your God will be with you wherever you go.

Then, when I did go anywhere, I would see these couples with a baby, or a mom holding her baby. I felt as if I was the only one without a baby.

Then I remember feeling guilty. Guilt in itself is enough without any other emotion tied into it. I would sit around whether I was alone or not and just doze off. Thinking, well, what did I do, could it have been because I smoked before I knew I was pregnant or maybe because I lay on the heating pad for my back, or no, maybe something I ate?

It might even have been whenever I stood in the chair to get a bowl from the upper cabinet. One night I even remember it was getting late so my mom went to bed and I was going to stay up and watch some TV.

A little while later I went upstairs to get some sweatpants out of my room.

When I was in my room I felt real eerie. So I quickly grabbed my pants and went back to the door towards the stairs and I felt as if someone was there when I looked behind me I saw a tiny black figure following me. The figure resembled a baby, only walking. I was so horrified, I couldn't even yell for my mother. I just started backing down the stairs thinking she's come to get me for what happened to her, it's my fault.

I was afraid to turn my back. I got to the bottom of the stairs and I backed all the way to the couch and sat there staring at the entrance to the stairwell waiting for it to come down after me.

Hours went by with my eyes wide open until I finally realized it was my mind playing tricks and I dozed off. That terrorized me for days, but has always haunted me.

(Psalm 23:4) As I walk through the valley of the shadow of death, I will fear no evil, for you my God are with me, your rod and staff they comfort me.

Then I felt ashamed. Ashamed that I had done something that could have caused this. That maybe I was not capable of having a baby. What if something was wrong with my baby ~ my body could not form a healthy baby, I was not worthy as a woman.

(Isaiah 50:7) Because the Lord helps me I will not be disgraced. Therefore I have set my face like flint and I know I will not be put to shame.

Confusion and anger then came to set in. These two play together because when you are confused about something you can't understand, it makes you angry. At first I thought this was just a freak accident, because the cord was around Kelsi's neck at delivery.

Then Dr. Amber called to check on me and to tell me that she got the pathology report on my placenta and it had ruptured and there was a blood clot at the top of the umbilical cord.

That means, in our English, that my placenta had torn loose from the uterus wall and then began to bleed and formed a blood clot at the umbilical cord, all of which cut off Kelsi's oxygen supply from me.

So that was the tearing feeling I had been having the night of my baby shower in the top of my stomach. So then I was confused because I couldn't figure out whether or not it was an accident or possibly some tests could have been done when I went to the hospital. Then that slammed me with anger to think that my baby could be alive if someone had not made a mistake.

(Eph. 4:26, 27) In your anger do not sin, do not let the sun go down while you are still angry and do not give the devil a foothold.

(Prov. 29:11) A fool gives full vent to his anger but a wise man keeps himself under control.

Many days went by; I had so much to think about. Sometimes I wanted to be alone to think without interruption. A lot of days I was so hurt and sad I didn't even get out of bed.

A lot of days I did get out of bed, but I never got

dressed. I had slipped into a depression.

All I wanted to do was sleep and when I did get up, I didn't eat much, just started smoking a lot. I had only hoped I would never wake up.

Sometimes, when I was awake I would be sitting on the couch and I would look down on the floor beside my feet and actually picture a baby carrier, but it always seemed to be empty.

I longed to know what it was like to care for a baby. The sleepless nights, crying, feeding, changing diapers and taking care of it when it's sick, and the cooing, cuddling and funny faces.

I was a total basket case. This was all in the first few weeks. I had no clue of what I was doing or what to do next. The counseling that my mom and I went to was helpful to some point, but I still felt disconnected.

There were many days that all the emotions you could possibly think of slammed me all at once. Those were the hardest times, you feel as if you will never come down off this emotional roller coaster.

Out of all of these emotions, there was one that had a more significant weight than all of the other emotions. One that never went away, and seemed to be suffocating me and that was ~ *EMPTINESS*.

Emptiness became my new way of life, no matter what I did, it consumed me. Being around all my family and friends, even going to church, nothing filled the emptiness in my chest.

All my life, I thought I was so tough that I could handle anything. I had been through some things when I was younger, some unspeakable events. I always got through them, what I thought was okay. But losing Kelsi before I ever got to really know her ~ this I was not ready for.

I was so lost and I was only getting deeper into my lost world. How would I ever learn to live again? Who would help me through this living hell? Who will fill my emptiness?

Signs from God

***

As I look back over my life at that time, there were many remarkable events that happened that only God could have pulled off.

As I said before, I was so lost that I knew if ever I would make it through, it had to be through God. When Mike left to go back up North and I felt that I needed to go and be with him. Somehow I felt he was my only connection to her because he was her father. So, a few weeks before I was scheduled to leave, my mom took me to the bookstore and let me pick out a new Bible. She wanted me to have whatever one I could read and understand.

So, I picked out the Rainbow Study Bible and I briefly began the next few weeks getting familiar with it. I knew that if I were going to find any answers to some of my questions, surely they would be in my Bible. The very first sign that I recall now, was when I was in the hospital. Before any of this happened, Mike and I had been deciding on names for a boy or a girl. I remember for a boy we had decided on Dustin and for a girl he wanted Chelsi and I wanted Kelsi. So after everything happened, the last thing on my mind was a name.

But, I recall the nurses coming in and out with papers as they do to read and sign and one nurse came in and she said, "Your boyfriend filled out the paperwork for you and you two chose Chelsi for the name, correct?" I never even thought about what anyone wanted or asked anyone, but out of my mouth came,

"No it's Kelsi. K-E-L-S –I." She changed it immediately. I didn't find out until later when my mom took me to the bookstore to buy a Bible what her name meant. You know how those bookstores have all those other goodies to look at. I was browsing through the name cards just to see if they had her name and they did.

And low and behold what it meant:

Kelsi ~ means "refuge" (Psalms 121) "I lift up my eyes to the hills – where does my help come from? My help cometh from the Lord, Maker of Heaven and Earth. He will not let your foot slip. He who watches over you will not slumber. The Lord watches over you. The Lord is your shade at your right hand. The sun will not harm

you by day, nor the moon by night. The Lord will keep you from all harm – he will watch over your life. And your coming and going both now and forever more."

WOW! When I read all that, that really grabbed my heart. Her name was chosen from the beginning because God knew her destiny. Notice that she also was born on January 21 (1:21). God surely was in control all along.

(Jeremiah 1:5) "Before I formed you in the womb I knew you, before you were born I set you apart, I appointed you as a prophet to the nations."

The name he chose was to give me direction to look to him for my help. Little did I know what all God had to tell and show me! The very next sign from God was the most remarkable.

My sister Denise and I had been out that day, what we had been doing, I don't recall. Denise probably just took me out shopping or something to get me out of the house.

I remember coming in late that evening and I went up to my room. My mind was just racing about so many things. At the hospital they had given me a large packet of things that belonged to Kelsi. Such as her little cap, her shirt, blanket and birth certificate, with her little footprints on it. I wanted so badly to smell her.

You know the sweetness of a new baby. Then I thought that since her feet actually touched this hospital certificate, surely her smell would be on it. So I reached for the packet and took out the certificate. I ran my fingers across the lock of black hair that had been cut from her and taped to the paper and then I lifted it to my nose to smell the footprints. Low and behold! The sweet scent that I encountered!

I was overwhelmed; the scent was just on where her feet had touched the paper. I was so excited. I ran downstairs with the certificate calling for my sister so she, too, could smell her footprints. She was in the kitchen and I told her what had happened and handed her the certificate to smell. She lifted it to her nose and smelt nothing, she said and tried again. Then she handed it over and said, "It must have been meant just for you." As I took it back and lifted it to my nose, the smell was no longer there.

I was devastated at first to know the only thing I had of my baby's smell was no longer there, but humbled that God was reaching out to me. At this point, I was ready to listen to God. He had my attention!

Sometimes God needs to speak to us in a way we can actually hear words. There were days that I was very quiet and to myself and some days I was talkative and didn't want to be alone. But, all the while, in my head, was a race and in my heart was like a puzzle of a million pieces. I was totally at a loss with empty arms. Here my body was going through all of these changes after having a baby; and for what? I had no baby to hold. My soul was quickly dying inside and I had no idea what trouble that can bring.

You see, when your soul begins to die, your hope for life, your will to fight and your faith in God also begins to die with you. Then the devil jumps in. Maybe with the thought of alcohol drowning your sorrow or overeating or sleeping all of the time or maybe even worse. All of these things are only downers ~ a temporary fix. Just remember that anything that can bring you down is from Hell. (Hell is down) Only God can bring you up. (Heaven is up).

Satan is a temporary fix. God is the everlasting life!
Permanent ~ Eternity.

**(John 10:27; 28) My sheep listen to my voice, I know
them and they follow me. I give them eternal life and
they shall never perish.**

The next significant sign from God was just that, him
speaking through someone's voice. One Sunday I went to
church with my mom. The pastor there was Reverend
Clark; he had known our family for quite sometime. He
was also the Reverend who performed Kelsi's funeral
service. He was the type of preacher who was really in
touch with God and shouted his word.

After his sermon this particular Sunday he said he
wanted everyone to close their eyes and bow their heads
and no looking around. So we did. Then he said; there is
someone here that is lost and doesn't know which way to
go! Raise your hand! My hand flew up like a kite. He
said, as if he already knew it was me before I raised my
hand, "Everything is going to be okay. God will guide you,

listen to him, he's with you." At that point I did not hear anything else he said because I was crying beyond control. *Who am I?* That he would care about me to stop this pastor's sermon for a special message through him to me!

I had never done anything to deserve his love. At that moment, as bad as my heart ached with pain and trying to make sense of it all, I knew God would love me through it and maybe help me to understand. I had no choice, but to listen, I did not want to live my life in deep heartache.

Who am I? I am a lost sheep and Jesus is my shepherd!

(Ezekiel 34:12 & 16) As a shepherd looks after his flock when he is with them so will I look after my sheep. I will rescue them from all the places where they were scattered on a day of clouds and darkness. I will search for the lost and bring back the strays. I will bind up the injured and strengthen the weak.

Let's just stop right here and take a few moments, read this again and then please join with me in prayer. For those of you reading this book you either are in the same shoes as me or know of someone who is. If it is you pray for yourself. If it is for someone you know, stand in the gap for them and pray for them to find healing in God.

Dear Father,

We come to you tonight in awe of you, your almighty sufficient grace and love. We thank you for loving us, even though we may not feel worthy, in your eyes we are. We pray today God that you would continue to pour out your power and love in our lives and overwhelm us with your peace. Help us to always seek your face even on the days we see no hope, breathe your spirit upon us, renew our minds, help us to understand we may never on earth know why our babies are not here, but that you God can fill our arms with love and our hearts with peace and serenity. We pray that nothing lead us astray. We rebuke anything Satan may try to offer. You God are our strength and our song. We praise you! In Jesus name Amen!

(Matthew 18:19-20) Where two or more come together in his name, whatsoever they ask, they shall receive.

Please feel free to pray this prayer, anytime, add to or change the words ~ but just pray. It may not seem like much to do, but it will change your world. Sometimes it takes time to feel better, but don't give up on God, even though sometimes he may be silent, he has a plan. Sometimes you have to allow your heart and mind to grieve and hurt so it may heal not just correctly, but thoroughly. So trust God.

There were many other signs in my days that I knew were from God. There have been times when I have been out to the cemetery and saw sparkles in the air right above Kelsi's monument. I call it angel dust. Another time I was really upset and just needed some peace on my heart. I had balloons in my hand, it was her birthday and I always release the number of balloons that would correspond to how old she would be that year. It was one of those times I asked God just to send me a sign, just something to give me some peace at that moment.

Suddenly these birds were flying overhead and one bird zeroed in on me and just soared directly above Kelsi's monument for several minutes then flew so close to me I thought he was going to pop the balloon. Immediately I felt peace.

There are some signs that God gives you and they are meant for only you. Just enjoy them. They are so special.

(Isaiah 7:11) Ask the Lord your God for a sign whether in the deepest depths or the highest heights.

(Isaiah 7:14) Therefore the Lord himself will give you a sign.

You will know when God is speaking to you. Usually you start to feel anxiousness in your heart and then it spreads to your chest and it feels like your heart is racing out of your chest. Whatever it is at that very moment, which is what God is convicting you of whether it be something he's trying to tell you or something you need to do or hear. Stop and listen. That is the spirit of God trying to reveal something to you. Do not be afraid.

(Romans 8:26 & 27) [26] **In the same way, the Spirit helps us in our weakness. We do not know what we ought to pray for, but the Spirit himself intercedes for us through wordless groans.** [27] **And he who searches our hearts knows the mind of the Spirit, because the Spirit intercedes for God's people in accordance with the will of God.**

This verse in the Bible basically means that there are times we are full of so much pain we have no idea where and what to start praying for......

(Psalms 46:10) Then you just be still and know that he is God.

God knows your heart. Remember Jesus "Son of God" suffered and died on the cross and if you believe in the cross then you believe that God knows our suffering. At that moment that you have no clue what to pray for but you know that is all you can do. Just go somewhere quiet and ask God to help you, for you are overwhelmed and at a loss for words. He will take it from there.

**(Habakkuk 2:10) But the Lord in his Holy Temple,
let all the earth be silent before him.**

God likes us to be silent sometimes, to humble
ourselves. There is a lot that can happen in silence, and
sometimes we may miss it by talking too much.

There will also be times in your life that you feel like
you're really through much of your grieving; you have
learned to live with it. But then you may be faced with a
situation that you never thought you would be in and you
are not dealing with it very well.

In my case it had been about four years. At that point in
my life I was happy. I was married and had another baby.

My husband, Mark was a shop foreman in an
automotive shop and was underneath a vehicle and pulled a
disc out of place in his neck. Well without getting into
great detail, he ended up having surgery. Of course, his
doctor was affiliated with the hospital I had delivered Kelsi
in. The hospital I swore I would never set foot in again.

Just because of the memories. Oh God how could this be? How was I going to deal with this?

Sitting around in this hospital while he was in surgery then spending the night! Well, I tried to focus on why we were there instead of my haunting past. His family was with me while he was in surgery so that wasn't so bad. Then, later after surgery, he was put in a room.

It was getting late and he was in bad shape so everyone left. I was afraid, afraid of not only being able to take care of him but also my own deeper fear. But later that night, when things were quiet, my mind began to replay every detail of that haunting day.

From being wheeled into the hospital admission, the tears, the nurses, the delivery and the silence of no baby crying, then the emptiness and I was overwhelmed with emotions once again...... there I was.

I felt as if I were in a cage and could not get out. I just lay there on my cot crying silently.

Once again in a silent hell I thought I had overcome. Then Mark was hungry so I went out into the halls searching for the nurse's station, realizing what floor we were on was the floor I was on after I delivered Kelsi. Before I knew it, I found myself wandering around the halls in the middle of the night, looking for the room I was in, as if I could remember the number.

Then I realized if the nurses began to pay attention to me, they might think I was some kind of psycho. So I made myself go back to the room. I was there to help my husband and I did, but all the while he was lying there in a physical painful hell, I lay on the cot next to him in a mental painful hell.

I could not wait to leave that hospital the next day. It was almost like getting out of prison. Now, I'm not going to say I ever overcame that because I still don't want to go back to that hospital, but I did learn something very important.

God revealed that to me because as I said you never get over a loss, you just learn to deal with it, and move on. I thought I had overcome every obstacle that there could possible be concerning the death of Kelsi. But God had to bring me face to face with what he knew I could not deal with, so I would realize I'm not above his guidance.

I'm sure with me and with you that there will be more obstacles to face, only fewer as the years go by. So see there are some signs from God we really don't want to experience. But, they will teach us valuable lessons. Nevertheless, good or bad, you will know when it is a sign from God.

Always remember there will be times of signs, which are not from God. When something happens and you are afraid for your life as if you want to run from it, it is not from God.

When it's from God, it can be overwhelming, awesome, wonderful, peaceful, and sometimes even a difficult lesson. Ask God for guidance if you feel like you cannot determine his signs.

(John 4; 1&2) Do not believe every spirit; test the spirits to see if they are from God. Every spirit that acknowledges Jesus Christ is from God. If not, it is not from God.

You will feel it in your heart ~ When it is from God!

Find things that will help you cope and move forward. For me when Hanna, Mike's sister in law gave me that mother owl figurine, it really gave me hope. On her first birthday my family bought me things for her. It was really sweet, but I had no place to keep the stuff.

So I bought a Curio cabinet and filled it with things that everyone bought for holidays and her birthday every year. It really helped me in the healing process.

I think this helped my family as well, with a sense of belonging.

Shout to the Lord

***

There are all different kinds of people in this world. People deal with things in different ways. Some people may decide they don't want to talk about the situation, that by talking about it, it only prolongs the pain.

These people feel better dealing with it silently. They still can't do it alone; they must confide and trust in God. It is okay if this person does not want to verbally express to others how they may feel, but it is never good to keep things "bottled" forever.

If you know someone like this, the best thing you can do is pray daily that they will seek God in their time of trouble and God will take it from there. God will find someway or someone to intercede with this person to heal their pain.

(Psalm 50) Call upon me in your day of trouble, I will deliver you and you will honor me.

Then there are some people that want and need to talk about it daily. They feel comfort and a sense of meaning to be found. That's great: all their feelings are being expressed. That is a great beginning to healing, not holding anything in. If you know someone like this, the best thing you can do is listen.

If it becomes an obsessive thing in other words, if the person never speaks of anything else, then you may try diverting the conversation to some other subject, but do so delicately. If no success, then you might want to try a professional counselor to help them deal with it. These people can also benefit greatly from a support group. All of this is good, and will take place in due time.

But we need to remember where to look for our help (Psalm 121) and to whom to give thanks and depend on.

(Psalm 147:3) The lord heals the broken-hearted and binds up their wounds.

(Matthew 5:4) Blessed are those who mourn for they shall be comforted.

Now, you can sit there day after day, sleep and dwell on it. That may happen for a time. But there needs to come a day that you get tired of the cycle and you want to break it. Believe me, listen closely, read this book again if need be. But, start with God. Pick up that Bible; pray to God for his help, he will not forsake you.

(Joshua 1:5) I will never leave you or forsake you.

I live my life today: a new person. I owe all I am, all I have, and all I ever will be to God. The way I see it is I could have lain there day after day. Or I could pick up what of me was left and give it to God to shape.

(Isaiah 64; 8) You are our father, we are the clay you are the potter. We are all the work of your hand.
(Jeremiah 18:6) Like clay in the hand of the potter so are you to mine.

See God wants us to understand and he wants to help us. But we have to want his help. He's ready and waiting, he's suffering over your suffering. Trust him to remold and shape you. I look at my life now and look at my life then and see so many times God has intervened and the times I tried to fix my own problems and they turned out even worse. Every time God intervened and I stayed out of the way, things were so much better.

My life now is a miracle because it is a miracle anyone can get through any tragedy. I remember all those days that I lay there crying myself to sleep, not eating, and not wanting to do anything because my heart was crushed and my soul was quickly dying. I knew then that I didn't want to live that way forever. It hurt too badly. I wanted the pain over and I knew only a man nailed to a cross to suffer and die, only to rise again, could be my hope.

He had the power to be resurrected and that is what I needed, a resurrection, a rebirth, because my soul was dead, my spirit broken.

(Psalm 51:17) The sacrifices of God are a broken spirit, a broken and contrite heart.

At that moment I began to pray, listen and learn. Many days and years have passed. I still miss Kelsi greatly. I love her and long to see her face. But, I no longer dwell on it. What I mean by that is I live my life and I focus on God first and he puts everything else in order.

I remember so well right after Kelsi died, the way that I felt. Alone, helpless, lost and it felt like I would always feel that way. I use to think that there could not possibly be anything in this world that could ever change the way that I felt. I thought I would feel that way forever. It felt like the end of the world and I wanted it to be. All I could see was the fact that I loved my baby so much and I wanted her greatly and I missed her so bad it was unbearable.

Somehow when I started to read my Bible daily, I began with Proverbs, why, I don't know, but that book of the Bible really pertained to my life at that time.

Things did not change right away and the pain didn't go

away. But I did begin a new focus and that was hearing what God had to say. Days and days went by and I continued to read as much as I could. That's whenever I started receiving signs and messages from God.

Now, I had never known what it actually felt like to have a relationship with God that you actually could feel his spirit and know this sign was from him. It is the greatest and most uplifting feeling in this world. My life did eventually change, with a lot of effort on my part, but it all took time and sometimes that alone is hard to deal with. But remember, God has perfect timing.

(Acts 1:7) It is not for you to know the times or dates the father has set by his own authority.

God knows our future, our needs and our wants. He also knows when our wants are not the right timing for our needs. He is in control of that. Trust him with it. It is hard when what you need or want is right now.

When you want your pain to be over, you need your pain gone.

Remember there is a time for everything:

(Ecclesiastes 3) A time to be born, a time to die, a time to weep, a time to laugh, (and if you just can learn to be patient and trust God.)

(Ecclesiastes 3:11) He has made everything beautiful in its time.

Now, I never said it was going to be easy. Learning to forgive Mike for all we had been through during our relationship and with Kelsi, also forgiving the doctor (for what I thought was her fault) and mostly learning to live with empty arms was the hardest thing I have ever had to do. Giving birth to Kelsi and knowing she was not going to cry or breathe was the hardest, unbearable, unspeakable thing I could have ever lived through. But I did ~ now that I have given all this to God and all I have trusted him with over the years.

Today I praise God because I no longer live in the darkness, the hell my life had become. My heart does not feel shattered anymore. Every breath that I take I don't wish to be my last. The wonderful things God has done for me I will speak of forever. I will shout to the Lord my praises of his glory. Mountains have bowed down in my life and seas have roared at the sound of God's name. God's power is so overwhelming; it's a promise of light, life and hope.

He has taken my empty chest that my shattered heart dwelled in and filled it with serenity, peace and joy. My mind that was misplaced he has filled with knowledge of his power and love. Into my empty arms he has filled with another child and my shattered broken soul he has filled with his spirit. With all that he has done and given me, how could I not praise him?

He is my rock and my salvation; I will live for him and praise his name forever.

You too can have these things, God's waiting for your call, and he loves you and wants so much to mend your broken heart. He is the living water, your thirst he can quench, trust and believe in him. You, too, one day will feel the way I do. Like standing on top of a mountain to sing of his glory and power and praise his name. One day when Jesus does return to take his followers home, we will be ready and we will be with our babies in heaven. Our babies that Jesus has rocked and held will be waiting. What a glorious day that will be.

Now there are many things that happen in this world that are trials and tribulations. There are times we hear of a divine intervention and sometimes we don't. The struggle comes when the events are happening to you and you don't know why. The only thing that keeps me on track during these times is the fact that our God is bigger than any problem we will ever have.

(John 16:33) I have told you these things, so that in me you may have peace. In this world you will have trouble. But take heart ~ I have overcome the world.

We live in an unjust world, a world of sin, sickness and disease. During these times it seems the hardest to believe that God is right.

That is where Satan wants us: questioning the will of God. That is when we really need to get on our knees and pray for guidance and deliverance from Satan's plan of destruction.

(John 1:29) Behold the Lamb of God – who takes away the sin of the world.

We must learn to be patient on his timing. God is in control although we may not understand why our babies died. If we knew the answer to every question we have, we would not lean on God as we should.

There are some things God may want us to know the answer why and some things we will never know. You may think that you will never find an end to ease your pain from the death of your baby unless you know why. Or you may already know exactly why and you're filled with anger.

But, that is the beauty of the lord. He can take a broken heart and mend it, he can take anger and turn it into compassion, and he can take confusion and turn it into serenity; if you let him.

Believe me because I was filled with all of these things,

anger, confusion, guilt, hurt and more.

Now after believing and trusting God with my life and living for God. His spirit has filled me with an overwhelming sense of peace with Kelsi's death, love, forgiveness, joy and serenity.

Often it brings a tragedy in our life before we are ready to see, feel or listen to God. But God is always waiting and always willing. There are still things that I face until this day concerning her. They are not easy, but God always helps me through. I remember on the very day that my doctor told me that Kelsi was dead, and I was beside myself, uncontrollably crying and I was in her office and she stepped out to get a nurse. I was pacing the room, my mind was racing, and my heart was breaking.

I stopped to look out of the window. I did not see anything, nor did I hear anything, but I briefly stopped crying ~ and something inside of me just knew "this was going to be... buckle up!" That could have been God's way of letting me know that this would come to pass! But, I didn't want to believe it. I had never known anyone that had ever been pregnant and their baby died. I didn't even know that was possible. The womb was supposed to be the safest place for a baby.

I remember my mom asking me if there was something the doctor could do. I remember my sister praying that "God would take this cup away!" (Biblical term) But not once do I remember praying for God to give her breath. Not that I didn't want that more than anything, to hear her suddenly cry. I knew that this was going to happen and somehow I was going to have to do this, deliver her, bury her, and learn to live without her. I couldn't just close my eyes and never wake up again. I tried, it's not that easy.

Bad things like this don't happen to bad people or good people, they happen to everyone! Christians too! When you become a Christian, it doesn't mean you become perfect like God.

You're still going to do things you shouldn't do, and, yes bad things will still happen.

(Ecclesiastes 9:11) The race is not to the swift or the battle to the strong nor does food come to the wise or wealth to the brilliant or favor to the learned: but time

and chance happen to them all.

When you become a Christian, you know where your source of help comes from and where to go for guidance and forgiveness when you get off track…God. The reasons for tragedies in life are not always going to be clear. But, you must be careful, sometimes trying to find a reason to our "whys" can consume you, sometimes finding out something before its time can destroy you. Ask God to help you with that, he will give you what you need to know, he won't give you more than you can stand, and he knows your strength.

(Psalm 139) Oh Lord, you have searched me and you know me, you know when I sit and rise, you perceive my thoughts from afar.

It's hard to believe that God could really know everything about each one of us. But he does, just read all of Psalm 139, and Jeremiah 1.

We as humans are not capable of the kind of love God

has for his children. We cannot comprehend that kind of love. It is way over our means of understanding.

(Isaiah 40:28) The Lord is the everlasting God, creator of the ends of the earth, he will not grow tired and weary, and his understanding no one can fathom.

(Proverbs 15:32) But he who heeds correction shall gain understanding.

Now, I have written a lot of poetry in my life, but I have never written a book. But, when God called me to write this book, I thought, "Man, you have to be kidding me!" But, hey Noah built an ark! He totally didn't know what he was doing. Noah is my favorite person in the Bible because of this.

Here he was a mere family man when God revealed to him he wanted him to build an ark. An ark of 75 feet in width, 450 in height. Where would he get his lumber? Where would he get his manpower to build such a boat? (Genesis 6:15) Just how would he get any wild animal to follow him on a boat? God chose Noah because he knew his inner strength.

He knew Noah would listen, and he did. Even as farfetched as it seemed, Noah trusted God's calling and God made the way for him to have what he needed to build this ark. Wow! Just imagine such a calling.

So, I knew if Noah could build an ark for his calling, I could write a book for mine, with God's help. Sometimes your calling could be out of the very tragedy you are in. One of the poems that I have written is a small poem, but very dear to my heart. …..

Witnessing a miracle is a life changing event
Becoming a miracle is a pure and true gift heaven sent

Now when you sit back at night watching TV and you hear of something great happening to someone, that had cancer and how they have overcome it and have an organization to raise money for victims and a self help for others, you think, "Wow, that's great." But nobody sits and prays, "Oh dear God I want to be a miracle?" Because you know to become a miracle you have to be ~ broken~

through some kind of tragedy ~ and nobody wants tragedy in his or her life, ever.

But I have become a miracle and that's why I say it's a pure and true gift heaven sent.

Why? Because there are lots of other things I could have become through my situation. Alone, a drug addict, an alcoholic trying to kill my pain, so many bad options. But, I chose to try God and trust him and he showed me love and filled my heart, mind, chest and life with his spirit and I began to breathe again. He lifted me up and we began to walk together and soon there were two sets of footprints in the sand.

I learned that even though Kelsi was my life and my child, she also was his child and she was in good hands and I learned to live with that. That is a miracle. That is truly a gift from God. Trying to understand why something happened will drive you crazy. Some people will even consume their selves with searching for an answer because it puts off dealing with the "acceptance." Sometimes, it is not meant for us to understand.

When we learn to change our focus from our problems

to God, it is only then that we will begin our journey with healing and receiving the peace of God.

(Philippians 4:7) And the peace of God that transcends all understanding will guard your hearts and your minds in Jesus Christ.

When you are distraught, no matter where you are, find a song or favorite Bible verse, something that draws you near to God.

Close your eyes sing the song loud or silent, just draw yourself into his presence, think about his arms wrapped around you and that everything is so peaceful there and you will begin to focus on that peace, the peace of God. More and more you will find yourself going there. So often when we are in pain, all we can see is the problem. That is understandable for a time.

There is always a time for mourning. We cannot make it a lifestyle, do not give in to depression. That is why it is important to refocus our mind, change our thoughts. Seek God in our pain; make yourself do what you don't want to do! If you don't feel like going to church, *go anyway!* If you don't feel like reading a verse from the Bible, *read it anyway!* Do something to change your focus! Soon you will begin to feel God's power overwhelm you and drive away the emptiness inside.

Remember **(Psalms 51; 17) The sacrifices of God are a broken spirit, a broken, contrite heart.**

At that moment that you find yourself ~ curled up in a ball, your eyes swollen from crying for days and your head is pounding from the frequent screams you express and your stomach is in knots from barely any food, on top of your nerves being wired and you find yourself begging for God to take your life. You can't set one foot in front of the other and every time you open your eyes after you have almost calmed down, reality sets back in that you're still here in your private hell. And you begin screaming again.

Right then, right there, in your "broken spirit" God is! God "is" taking your life, only not the way you have in mind. He is taking your life in his hands; in his control.

(Psalms 107:13) They cried to the Lord in their trouble and he saved them from their distress. He brought them from their distress. He brought them out of darkness and the deepest gloom and broke away their chains.

My pastor often says: To have a victory, you must have a battle. When we begin to let go and experience God's power and blessings, our private hell is not as deep, we don't stay there as long and it's easier to get out, when we trust in God. God never said this world would be easy. If you read through your Bible, you will see even from the beginning of time there was always some kind of trouble, family trouble, trouble with nations, trouble of every kind and sickness.

(Deuteronomy 20:4) For the Lord your God is the one who goes with you to fight for you against your enemies to give you victory.

I cannot tell you why things happen. No one can. I cannot tell you why God intervenes in certain situations and others he doesn't. The only explanation I could ever make sense of is the fact that we live in an unjust world of sin, killing, robbery, sexual abuse, child abuse, mental abuse, even religious abuse and much sickness and disease. People make choices; they make their own decisions instead of seeking God and asking for his direction in life. Then they get destruction in their lives. Remember no matter what takes place in your life…

(Jeremiah 29:11) God still has a plan for you.
(Hebrews 11:40) God had planned something better for us so that only together with us would they be made perfect.

Key word: Together!! Just remember there is beauty in this world. If you are out of God's will for your life he will arrange circumstances to put you back on his track. Just believe and trust him. There is no telling what his plan is for you.

Let's look at Moses. (Exodus) Pharaoh had ordered the death of every baby boy. Moses parents hid him for 3 months, then put him in a basket and sent him down the river. Pharaoh's daughter found him. It was God's plan for Moses to be raised by Pharaoh. As Moses got older he saw an Egyptian beating a Hebrew, one of his own people. Moses got angry and took things into his own hands and killed the Egyptian (at that moment he stepped out of God's will). Moses then ran away, afraid. He lived in a place called Midian where he met his wife and lived herding sheep for a long time.

Until one day God was ready to approach Moses so he did, through a burning bush. He told Moses what to do, Moses doubted, but he led Moses and it was a very long and hard journey, but through Moses, God set the people free. Read the story, it is truly amazing. What's truly amazing is a lot of us are just like Moses. By one simple act, not even knowing we step out of God's will.

Then we know we are in trouble and our first instinct is to run and hide. We live in a place like Midian for quite some time. See, God never leaves us; sometimes he just gives us some room to breathe, think and grow, like he did with Moses. Then he will reveal his will to us. Just listen and obey, don't be afraid of failure. God will lead you through every brick wall you come up against. Develop your faith in God: The definition of faith is believing what you can't see and knowing it's real. Read Hebrews 11, faith is defined and illustrated through the lives of Old Testament heroes. These people were very strong and courageous, but also human, like us.

Some of them made mistakes; some took things into their own hands, why, because they began to lose their faith. That is very easy to do when it takes a long time. We as humans are not good with time, we want it now! If there were immediate action we wouldn't learn to trust God, develop and grow.

None of this, however, will come to pass unless we make the decision to accept God's will for our life. It will involve doing things you have never done. Like giving up your comfort zone, stepping out in faith, letting go of the past and mostly trusting God and waiting time. Counting the years it has been since my daughter, Kelsi has passed away. The first year was horrible. I remember every detail of that day. The second birthday was also horrible. I remember every detail of that day. The third year was bad, but not quite as bad as the first two. The fourth year was like a reality that this was my life. The fifth year was all right. I had learned to deal with her birthday quite well.

The sixth year was the same. The seventh year was different. It was a very bittersweet day for me! On her seventh birthday, I just thought about the celebration she was having in Heaven. Her days are endless there. Her days are beautiful, painless and free. That is all a mother could ask for her child. That makes me happy for her.

I think my worst is, Christmas Day. I often wondered of the joy that I could see with Kelsi and my daughter Morgan as they opened Santa's gifts. I usually ended up in the shower for a long heartfelt cry. There will always be days like that for years to come. Now each year that has passed has not been easy, but another stepping stone in my life. I really don't like to go to the cemetery on January 21 of every year. That was not my plan; but that is my life. It was very hard at first, but as time passed, it got easier.

Trust me ~ there are still times that really get me upset even now. *Tears cleanse the soul.*

In 2005 I became pregnant again. I was so excited as I had wanted another child for many years and Morgan was now 10 years old. Things were ok and I made it to my third month before any issues started. I went to the doctor (alone) for my check up only to be told my baby had no heartbeat. Long story short, I lost that baby as well. No conclusion as to why. So the doctor scheduled a DNC to remove the baby that was no longer breathing. This was like a cruel replay of before; thankful I was just 3 months this time. I remember getting in the car after leaving the office and driving in a daze, then to pull over to just be hit by reality this was happening again! It hurt so deeply as it peeled open all those old wounds. And trying to explain to Morgan was very sad, but being so early in my pregnancy she didn't have an emotional connection. This was very hard for me to accept as I felt not capable as a woman. This was the last time I would ever be pregnant.

Although I had a successful birth with Morgan, I myself had complications after her delivery. I will never know why I had these problems during pregnancy. It's just a part of my life that I had to learn to deal with. Sometimes I still don't accept it. But I talk myself out of the crazy thoughts that sometimes consume me. I never let those thoughts linger very long as they can create a bondage. I quickly control them: as they don't DEFINE me!!

(Colossians 3:2) Set your minds on things above, not on earthly things.

(2 Timothy 1:7) For God gave us a spirit NOT of fear but of power, love and self-control.

(Proverbs 4:23) Keep your heart with all vigilance, for from it flow the springs of life.

Even though I never had the chance to have any more children, I am lucky enough to have many nieces and nephews. I have a very strong bond with most of them, to include a few of my daughter's closest friends. They are all a HUGE part of my life. Even though it does not replace the bond of a mother and child; they have been my saving grace.

I often think about how different things would be in my life if Kelsi was here.....

The way she would look, what her personality would be like. If she would be like Morgan or total opposite, like most siblings. Would she be athletic or prissy?

Then I remember …. My God had an ultimate plan for her, far better than what I could have ever given her.

It's going to take time to heal, for some longer than others. Just remember **"there's mercy in the meantime."** Throughout these past years I have learned a lot.

That life isn't fair, but God is there.

Tears are always going to fall

But God always hears your call

There will be rainbows in the sky

There will always be questions why

There's mercy through God's Grace

There's victory through every trial we face.

Through God's mercy and grace he has helped me through every sad moment, every time I replay that day like a broken record, every time I begin to lose sight of him and every time I begin to doubt:

(Titus2:11) For the grace of God that brings salvation has appeared to all men.

(Titus 3:7) Having been justified by his grace we might become heirs having the hope of eternal life.

(Isaiah 30:18) Yet the Lord longs to be gracious to you. He rises to show you compassion. For the Lord is the God of justice. Blessed are all who wait for him.

(2 Corinthians 12:9) My grace is sufficient for you, for my power is made perfect in weakness.

(Isaiah 63:9) In all their distress, he too, was distressed, and the angel of his presence saved them. In his love and mercy he redeemed them; he lifted them up and carried them all the days of old.

No matter what you are facing and dealing with today, God's grace and mercy are with you. God hurts when you hurt. His promises are real and true. You have nothing more to lose. Learn to trust in him. Reach out today and let him heal your pain and broken heart. <u>No medicine can do that. But through God, you will be healed.</u>

(Isaiah 53:5) He was pierced for <u>our</u> transgressions. He was crucified for our iniquities. The punishment that brought us peace was upon him and by his wounds we are healed.

God had to love us to watch his only son be beaten and nailed to a cross to suffer and die for our sins. His promise to us is peace; through his wounds we are healed.

(Psalms 147:3) He heals the broken hearted and binds up their wounds. Has a doctor ever told you that? I didn't think so.

(Exodus 15:26) For I am the lord who heals you.

Throughout my time of learning to deal with Kelsi dying, I found a lot of my answers in the Bible. I simply looked up in the index what I was feeling at that moment and began to read. Then I began to trust and believe and give my burdens and pain to God. Then my life started to change. My focus became to heal my pain, not to dwell in my pain. It wasn't easy; it took much dedication.

You know, I realized that I could write this book forever on God's Glory; trying to make you realize that your pain does not have to be your own. At some point you have to take the first step.

I will always remember the sheet covering her face. But now I have God's grace. I will always remember the tears in my family's eyes, but now I have a rainbow in my skies. I will always remember the emptiness that consumed me. But through God, my heart has been set free.

You also will always remember these things, but it is up to you to have God's grace in your life, to receive a rainbow in your sky, to have your heart set free of that clinching pain that can destroy you and everyone around you. Remember that you are not just affecting you, but all those around you, as well.

Think about how you want people to look at you. Make a decision to trust God and believe in his word, then live it and display God's grace in your life to others with your words and actions. Show the world how God has overcome your pain. The choice is yours.

God is every reason for *"everything"* that I am and have today. I praise God in all that comes my way.

He has taken every broken piece to my body and soul and made me whole again. Today I can firmly plant my feet on the ground and say that I am victorious through God. I have won this battle!

My hope and prayers are for all of you who have experienced any sort of infant loss, to find peace. It is a horrific loss to go through. A rose pulled before its time. Let that rose blossom in your heart. I hope that you can find your answers the way that I did, through God's word. God will love you through this like no other can. Make time to read the Bible during this journey.

(2 Timothy 3:16) All scripture is God-breathed and is useful for teaching.

<u>There is also a lot of beauty to see in this world:</u>

Endless oceans.

Majestic mountains.

The burst of colors in the sky at dusk.

The brightness of dawn.

The wind that chases the butterflies through open fields.

Dandelions blowing in the wind.

Find the things that give you peace and comfort. Share your thoughts with others, this sometimes is more helpful than you can imagine.

Find your comforting tools and use them as you need them. There will be brighter days ahead!

~ Life Tip: Never let the actions or inactions of a person or a bad situation create the path you are on. You <u>control</u> the outcome, you <u>define</u> your destiny and you <u>create</u> your story.

Dealing with a Sibling

***

Morgan is my only child now; she was born December 29, 1995, almost exactly 2 years later from Kelsi, who was born January 21, 1994. It helped me greatly; she is the joy of my life. Through the years, she has been with me to visit her sister at the cemetery.

Along with other things she had picked up on. I never wanted to hide it from her, because I did not want to hide Kelsi away from our world. This is just the way I chose to deal with it at the time. Sometimes I wonder and really think whether I made a mistake by letting Morgan know about Kelsi so young. Morgan had a lot of questions that were sometimes hard for me to answer.

I have never let her see me cry about Kelsi. But, children are not stupid; they feel the sadness of someone that is supposed to be there but is not. Death is all a part of life. Morgan mostly missed Kelsi because she would have been a playmate at that point in her life. Any questions that Morgan asked me, I answered only on her level and did not offer any more information. I talked to my pastor about it because I was afraid I had made a wrong decision by ever letting her know.

He advised me that it is a part of our life and death is in this world. That by answering her questions on her level was the best thing that I could do. We cannot shield our children from this world. It is not possible. They are going to find out sooner or later. So, if you have other children go to God in prayer and ask for his help on how you should handle the situation of revealing or keeping it from them.

Also, remember how it will help you to deal with the loss. If your child is older, answer their questions to their age level. Seek advice if needed. This could be very traumatic for a child that has experienced the whole ordeal with you. Let them express their feelings to you if they want to. When Morgan asked who Kelsi was, I simply explained to her that at one time before she was born mommy was pregnant with another baby and at that time God needed some baby angels in heaven, so he took Kelsi to heaven to live. Someday, a long time from now, we would go to heaven to see her.

I left it at that. At that time she was four. I almost changed the subject and avoided the question, but then I was afraid that could cause her damage. It's like trying to put pieces of a puzzle together. When they're trying to figure out the next piece, they ask for help. You show them the piece, but let them put it together.

I may have been wrong to expose her, but she was a very happy little girl and God was in control of the situation. Every year, on Kelsi's birthday, Christmas, Easter and in the summer, Morgan and I would go to the store and pick out the best flowers then take them to the cemetery to place them in her vases. On Kelsi's birthday, we always bought the number of balloons of her age, write a letter and sent them to heaven for her party. That made Morgan happy. Whether you choose to reveal it now or when they're older, be ready, there will be tons of questions.

Just ask God the way you should answer the questions, he will guide you through.

~ (Romans 8:18) The pain that you have been feeling can't compare to the joy that is coming. ~

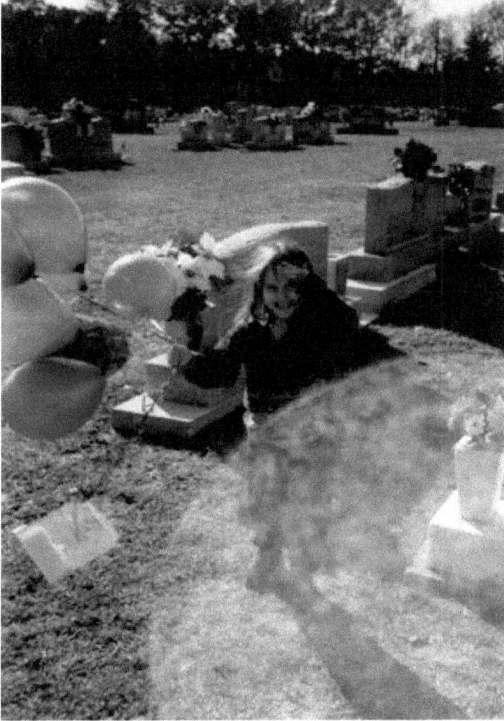

This is the letter Morgan wrote attached to the balloons to send to her party in heaven. It was always so bitter sweet, but brought much peace.

This is how we decorated out at the cemetery during holidays or for her birthday. Her monument is white marble with pink insert roses.

Thoughts from the Family

***

A Grandmothers Memory

When Nickie was carrying Kelsi I was so worried about her and her problems in her life; just as any other mother would be.

The connection with the baby at the time I did not feel real strong until the day Dr. Amber called me and said I needed to come to Nickie that her baby had died. I could hear Nickie in the background crying uncontrollably.

It was like something stabbed me in my heart for the pain was so real, when I held my granddaughter Kelsi the day she was born. I can still see her now, feel her and smell her. She was so beautiful. I really do not know how Nickie dealt with it so well except by the Grace of God. I really do not know how to explain how I dealt with this loss.

I thought about how we would never see her grow up. And my arms would never hold her again. Then I would think about how she was a beautiful angel in Heaven with

Jesus. And I had to be strong for Nickie. I thank God for all that he done for Nickie. One of the things that helped me was that my mother had died one year before Kelsi and I kept telling myself that my mom was also with Kelsi and Jesus had great care of them both. I thank God for his love and mercy towards Nickie.

I do not know if I could have ever handled this if I were her. I am so proud of my daughter and I know God has something special for her.

**Grandma

An Aunts Memory

I am so sorry and will never forgive myself because I was not with Nickie the day she went to the doctor alone. I had gone with her many times before. I can not find the words to say how bad I feel that she was alone. And why we did not know that something was wrong the night she went into labor. And why we did not know that something was not right with the pain she was having. I should have known to go with her to the doctor.

When she went to the hospital to give birth to Kelsi, it was the most special day in the whole world. I prayed so hard because I just knew that God could and would put life back in that tiny precious little body. She was so special in more ways than we could know at that time. We were unaware of what God's miracle was since the day she was conceived, because only God knew she was carrying a "Perfect Angel," that was meant to live in Heaven with him. Sort of like the way he chose Mary to give birth to his son Jesus. But even still this was a very traumatic time for the family. How she did it other than God's grace upon her that day.....

I will never know. I thank God for letting us see her in such great beauty; because of how we loved her. I remember standing in the hall and hearing someone talk about how she looked, describing her so differently than what I had seen. (Because she had been dead for several days, her body changed rapidly after the delivery.)

Then the day we went to the hospital to pick up the pictures the hospital had taken, I could not believe what I saw. It was not Kelsi. And I could not let Nickie see them.

Now I think back to how some people described her after she was born. Now I know that we saw her through God's eyes. And I thank God for letting us see her that way because we loved her so much. Sometimes when I think back, I wish I had held her for a little while.

Aunt Nini

An Aunts Letter

Kelsi,

Well where do I begin....?

I have so many things to say, and think of you often. I wonder if your hair is curly like your moms. Would you have brown eyes? But instead I know you will never know the joy of playing at the park with the sun on your face. Going to a sleep over at your "best friend's house, or sleeping over at Aunt Patsy's house. But I hope you know you are missed and loved a great deal.

Some days the pain feels like yesterday! I realize that I will never hold you or see you in a play at school. We will never get our pictures taken together and you won't go to the prom. I know God has far more for you than we could have ever given you. It's just my selfish thinking that gets the best of me sometimes. Kelsi, I am sure you know we never gave up hope thru the whole delivery that you would have breath in your body.

Only when the doctor placed you in the bassinet, she covered your face ~ I have never felt so alone as that day. My heart was broken... your mom was crushed!

I remember her words as she received the epidural: "Nothing can hurt me any more than I am already hurting." God's mercy was so real that day. As the nurse brought you in so we could see you, all we saw was a beautiful little angel.

I know I will see you again someday in Heaven. Until then, thank you for being our "Guardian Angel."

P.S. I see you swinging on the playground.

Love forever,

**Aunt Patsy

An Uncles Memory

I feel a special burden in writing this and expressing my feelings on how Kelsi's birth/death affected me. I always have thoughts, conscious and unconscious, about her when I look at my little boy Logan. I think about how she would look today, how tall she might be, how she might sound or walk in comparison to Logan. After all her and Logan would be the same age now.

Just thinking about her fills my eyes with tears. When I heard the news that Kelsi had died it was truly a shock. The deepest pain I can ever remember.

I have suffered much sadness and undesired surprise and loss throughout my lifetime. This by far was the worst. My heart was so heavy with sadness and concern for Nickie. The deep and unending pain she would suffer from now on.

This was possibly the worst loss we have ever experienced in our family. The fact that we would never get the chance to say we knew her personally and experienced her grandeur. This alone was hard enough to bare. I remember my first thought was to get to Nickie, hold her and cry with her. I could not do that because I was so far away.

When I finally did get to her I remember thinking I can not let her see my pain. I felt I needed to be strong for her. It is hard to really express such feelings of intense hurt. The void of Kelsi's life that is within my sisters will always and forever be also within me.

The strangest thing I remember about this experience may seem a little radical. I believe that during the minutes just before Kelsi's delivery was the first time I can recall actually feeling God's presence within me. I believed that God delivered a message to me at that moment that Kelsi was born.

The message was that our child; Lyn's and mine, would be a boy. I believe the reason for that was to comfort Nickie and us. The feeling was surely awesome and yet frightening. It was though an actual being whisked through my body. It was like a breeze of strong air that passes you by briefly, only it was on the inside of me not the outside. I know this sounds unreal but it did happen to me while I was waiting out in the hallway. Kelsi a girl and Logan a boy the difference would serve as a shield to comfort us all in some way.

I will never forget the painful time that my heart hurt out of sorrow and fear; the sorrow for Nickie's pain and the fear of our unborn child that we were also expecting. I had various thoughts about, could this happen to us? I also thought about how our presence near Nickie made her feel. I know Kelsi is even more beautiful in Heaven.

Surely she is special, for God chose her. I know how I feel about my own children and the deep love I have for them. I can only imagine a part of how Nickie feels about Kelsi's death. I guess we will never know God's divine reason for taking her so early. I know we will always and forever have this burning question in our hearts and minds. I know she is in good hands and in a better place than we are. I let this fact comfort me each day. But I will always suffer with my sister.

**Uncle Bubba

A Best Friend's Sorrow

When you have a friend that is so dear to your heart as Nickie is to mine, the last thing you want to see them go through is the death of a child. The death of a child is the most devastating and heart wrenching feeling any human being could fell. I blamed myself at first, why I do not know.

I remember thinking, God why her? No one deserves this pain and suffering especially not Nickie.

I thought to myself, I have been blessed with two beautiful and healthy daughters, and another on the way. Why not take my unborn child instead of Nickie's baby. I can carry the pain, I am stronger. I prayed to God, please don't let this be. Nickie and I have been close friends since the age of nine. Nickie was the good one I was the one who made all the bad choices.

I always admired and respected her. So why did she have to endure such a tragedy? It should have been me not her. I would have given my soul to take her pain away and put everything back as it was.

The day Nickie went to see the doctor, I felt in my heart

that something was wrong. I wanted to go with her but she insisted she would be fine and was going alone. I did not know until later that my heart was telling me that she was going to need me more than ever, once she had seen her doctor. I went home from work a nervous wreck.

When the phone rang I knew what was going to be said, the baby was dead. The most important thing now was to go to Nickie, be her strength. I had to save her. But how was I going to do that? Even as great as my love is for her I knew I would not be able to say or do anything to ease her pain.

Nickie was told that she would have to deliver her baby the next day. I thought, how cruel to make her do this as if it was a normal birth knowing what the outcome would be. As much as I wanted to be there for her, I wanted to run just as fast from her. I had so much guilt for not being with her when she received the news and so many what ifs. I could not bear to see her in pain.

I really don't think any of us slept that night. The next morning was quiet because everyone knew what the day would bring.

We arrived at the hospital. They set everything up and began their procedure. I helped Nickie into her gown. I think I was like a mother hen trying to protect her chicks, but I could not help myself. I just wanted to take care of her. Make her whole. In my selfish mind I was the only one who could do that. I wanted to take her in my arms and hold her tight.

Tell her everything was going to be fine. I wanted to tell her that she could have my baby when it came, anything to save her. Then reality told me that no matter what I said I was not going to be able to make it better. No matter how bad I wanted to fight for her this was a battle we were going to lose. After what seemed an eternity, the time came to deliver the baby.

I remember thinking God please let this be some horrible mistake. Let this baby come out alive and crying. I held on to that thought to the very end. Until I seen her beautiful little face knowing we would not hear her cry. I knew her wonderful mommy was not going to be able to look her in the eyes. The room was so thick with pain you could have cut it with a knife. After they took Kelsi away I could not keep my eyes off of Nickie. I was waiting for her to lose it. I thought reality would set in and she would start to scream, lose control or maybe even lose her mind from the pain. She needed me and I was going to be there.

After a while I went downstairs, outside where I could breathe. I sat there thinking, praying for strength that the both of us needed. I asked God to forgive me for any and all wrong things I had ever done. I needed him, for my friend and myself. When I went back upstairs I knew it was time to say goodnight. I kissed Nickie and held her as tight as I could. I left the hospital that night dazed and confused. I needed God now to help her with what I could not do.

**Aunt Tanya

As you see, members of the family are also affected deeply by the death of an infant.

When my mother held Kelsi all she could think was that she would never again hold her grandchild. --- Now we know she was blessed to hold God's chosen angel.

When my sister Denise saw Kelsi --- she realized the beauty of seeing through God's eyes.

When Patsy's heart was burdened by Kelsi never being able to run and play in the park with the sun on her face. Little did she realize --- that Kelsi would be running in the park, "with God's SON."

When my brother felt a fear for his unborn child --- God quickly reminded him that he was in control.

When my best friend Tanya thought that she could make things better reality set in --- it brought her to her knees to seek for Gods help.

So after you have read their memory of that day you can see, the presence of God filled that delivery room.

In all the despair ~ in all the tears ~ in all the pain ~ and even within my shattered soul that was screaming inside.

God was there…. Holding our hands, touching our face and wiping our tears. We all felt God's presence and seen the face of an angel.

Special Poetry

***

These are a couple of poems that I wrote that give me great inspiration:

I hope they will inspire you as well……

At A Glance

At a glance, I saw your peaceful face.

I knew that another could never take your place.

At a glance, I knew that I would never hear you cry in the silence of the night.

My one precious memory is my mother's arms holding you tight.

At a glance, wearing satin and lace, you received your wings and were ready to fly.

But I just was not ready to say goodbye.

At a glance, as the tears fell upon my face.

I knew that heaven was a better place.

At a glance, I will never know the joy you would bring as I watched you grow.

Maybe blue eyes and curly hair, a stolen dream I will never know.

At a glance, I knew on earth you and I would never have another chance.

God's bittersweet gift to me was to carry an angel and one precious glance.

At a glance, the emptiness seeped into my chest as they took you away.

You slipped in and out of my life all in one day.

At a glance, I knew there had to be a reason WHY?

With these words, I love you Kelsi and I will never say goodbye.

Power and Promise

As I stand in your presence when I am called home.

My eyes can scarcely focus thru the gleam from your throne.

I hear the angels whisper all around.

In awe, I quickly kneel on your Holy Ground.

My earthly life flashes before my eyes.

I begin to receive the answer to all my "Whys?"

The pain and sin is wiped from my mind as you pour out your love.

As I stand flying above your throne is a dove.

Stepping down from your lap, my baby girl that has grown thru your care.

As she runs towards me and falls into my arms, my heart can hardly bear.

Your power, your promise, her face, her heart beating against mine.

And you say to me "No greater love than thine."

In the Arms of the Father

Thru the sorrow it's hard to see,

The beauty that can be within a tragedy.

The pain can keep a miracle in disguise.

In the arms of the Father, wipe the tears from your eyes.

Understanding will come when you humbly bow your
knee.

You will learn to accept what has to be.

His peace will overpower the anger inside.

In the arms of the Father, let him be your guide.

In time good things shall come of this.

In faith believe that God is in the midst.

Take to the altar what comes your way.

In the arms of the Father, let your burdens lay.

Those of you that have experienced this pain, I hope that in some way this book will inspire you to not only ***trust in God*** but to ***lean on him for your understanding***.

Although it is not easy and it takes time to heal. Remember…. there is *"nothing"* that is too big for our God to handle. I have grown in so many ways from her death and so has my family. You and your family can as well, with Gods grace.

We will always and forever have Kelsi's footprints implanted on our hearts……

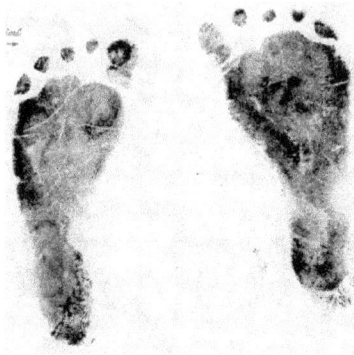

May God bless you always!

Journal Notes

Sometimes just getting things on paper is a huge help. Take some time to make notes of your experience and steps you can take to walk this journey.

What are some ways you are feeling?

_____

_____

_____

_____

_____

_____

_____

_____

_____

_____

_____

_____

What are some signs from God you have experienced?

_____

_____

_____

_____

_____

_____

_____

_____

_____

_____

_____

_____

_____

_____

_____

_____

What are some ideas you have to start your healing process?

_____

_____

_____

_____

_____

_____

_____

_____

_____

_____

_____

_____

_____

_____

_____

_____

_____

What are some things you can change in your thinking patterns in regards to this loss?

_____

_____

_____

_____

_____

_____

_____

_____

_____

_____

_____

_____

_____

_____

_____

_____

Bible verses that give you peace and comfort.

_____

_____

_____

_____

_____

_____

_____

_____

_____

_____

_____

_____

_____

_____

_____

_____

www.ingramcontent.com/pod-product-compliance
Lightning Source LLC
Chambersburg PA
CBHW060254050426
42448CB00009B/1635